FROM THE POINT TO THE CROSS

ONE VIETNAM VETS JOURNEY TOWARD FAITH

DEN SLATTERY

© 2004 by Den Slattery. All rights reserved.

No part of this book may be reproduced, stored in a retrieval system, or transmitted by any means, electronic, mechanical, photocopying, recording, or otherwise, without written permission from the author.

ISBN:1-4140-4315-5 (e-book)
ISBN: 1-4140-4314-7 (Paperback)

This book is printed on acid free paper.

Point to the Cross logo by Nancy Terryn of Pentwater, MI
In conjunction with Kwik Print of Ludington, MI

All photos by Den Slattery

1st Books - rev. 03/08/04

COMMENTS FROM READERS

"*From the Point to the Cross* is great! Your life and my own have paralleled in many ways. I pray that many copies of this book are distributed. It is so well written that I know many people will benefit from it."
    Merlin Carothers (Best Selling Author of *Prison To Praise*)

"Have enjoyed your book greatly. It is excellent!"
    Dr. Rose Sims (Author of *New Life for Dying Churches*)

"I loved Den's book. It was provocative. It would make a great movie."
    Bill Honer (Stock Broker—Traverse City, MI)

"The attitudes and perspectives of the times were so real in Den's book, that I could sense the heat of Vietnam and even remember the smells."
    Bill Mater (Former Mortician in Vietnam 1970)

"*From the Point to the Cross* grabbed my attention so strongly that I couldn't put it down. It is MUST reading! It made me stop and think a lot about my life and about Jesus Christ."
    Burt Stafford (Retired Farmer—South Bend, IN)

"After reading *From the Point to the Cross* I was inspired to change my life. I accepted Jesus Christ as my Savior and began to study the Bible and attend church. This has helped to fill a big void in my life. Thanks Den for sharing your life story."
    Jerry Altimus (Former pointman in Vietnam 1967)

"Den's book, *From The Point To The Cross,* was a jolt to my placid Christian life. I felt challenged when I realized where he had come from."
    Ann McCuistion (CPA—Jones, MI)

"Be encouraged Dad, I think you are great!"
    D.J. Slattery (Den's only son)

"I read Den's book , *From The Point To The Cross,* and then went out and bought two more copies to give away. It's a great book!"
      Peggy Sprague (Farmers wife/Dowagiac, Michigan)

"I'm not a big reader of books but I started to read your book and it was really interesting. I loved reading about your adventures in Vietnam and about how you came to know the Lord. It was amazing to see how God provided for you and answered your prayers. It truly gave me a great hope. I learned a lot from your book in every area and it has helped me to pray and to ask God to show me where He wants me in life and what my purpose is. I just thank God for giving that book to me."
      Paul Reid (College student in Dublin, Ireland--2003)

"I'm 16 and I live in Berry, New South Wales, Austrailia. I just finished reading your book, *From the Point to the Cross*. I've gone to Church my whole life but I never really made a commitment to God. I don't want to go to Hell. I want to believe. I have asked Jesus into my heart."
      Michael Bolt (16 year old from Australia)

"I really enjoyed reading *From The Point To The Cross.* What a marvelous story of God's faithfulness and provision."
      Greg Parris (Methodist Pastor in Muncie, Indiana)

"*From the Point to the Cross* makes good reading and gives glory to our Lord."
      Rev. Paul Johanson (President of Elim Bible Institute, NY)

"*From the Point to the Cross* is more than just another life story. It is a captivating account of a very brave man and his struggle with society, war, family, and faith. The text is riveting. It is written with both compassion and brutal honesty. Bravery allows the author to make admissions that many of us would not. I am extremly proud to have known Den and to be considered his friend."
      Major Jim Wilson (U.S. Army/Retired)

"*From the Point to the Cross* is a truly inspiritional book. A must for everyone who needs a boost in their faith. It is easy to read and enjoyable for both men and women."
Tom Jacobs (Chief of Police)

"I found myself encouraged and reassured of God's love as I read Den's book."
Debbie Floor (X-Ray Tech)

"*From the Point to the Cross* was very hard to put down once I started reading it. A very good book."
Helen Hewitt (Dowagiac, MI)

"Here is a book about finding a purpose in life that makes a compelling argument that God provides answers. Den Slattery invites the reader to share his remarkable experiences and His acceptance of Jesus Christ. An inspirational book for all."
Gary Huff (Vice President of Lyons Industries/SW Michigan)

"I enjoyed Den's book *From the Point to the Cross*. It was told from the heart and it reminded me of what God can do."
Elva Rose (Dowagiac, MI)

"Den's book gave me new hope. It reminded me that God is still drawing people to himself no matter what they've done. Once I started reading *From the Point to the Cross* I didn't want to put it down. It is a life changing book."
Debbie Sprague (Dowagiac, MI)

"*From the Point to the Cross* chronicles the experiences that shaped a man from a self-centered youth into a caring minister who knows his story is not done. Den shares in a straight-forward sincere manner the fear and terror of the frontline infantry soldier in Vietnam. Den's story touched my heart and revitalized my faith. I rejoice in the message it delivers."
Barbara Cox (Elementary Public School Principal)

"*From the Point to the Cross* is not a book to sit on your shelf. Read it and pass it on. It's message is deep and convincing."
    Dorothy Shug (Retired Public School Teacher)

"I found the book, *From the Point to the Cross*, very interesting to read. I pray it will be a blessing to many."
    Ron Griffin (Baptist Pastor—Jackson, MI)

"This book is a testimony of God searching for the lost and calling them to Himself. It is also the testimony of the radical change Jesus makes when we trust and obey."
    Bill Sprague (Fruit Farmer—Dowagiac, MI)

"I read Den's book from cover to cover in one night. It was very encouraging."
    Bruce Oliver (PA)

"We read this book as soon as we got it and we loved it. The Lord was lifted up and glorified throughout."
    Gary and Chris Lubitz (TX)

"I started reading your book as soon as I got it. . . I cannot believe how much faith you had after what you went through in your life. The best part of your book is the last chapter (Yellow Ribbons) because it is me to a TEE. I have had so many things happen to me over my life that I never had a thought as to how to get out of the mess I was in."
    Merle Grosjean (IN)

"Your book arrived on Friday afternoon and I laid in bed on Saturday morning until I finished it around 10:30 AM. I really enjoyed it. . . Your testimony is incredible. . . you have so much to offer others. Your life has been rich with experiences. I'm including a yellow ribbon in this envelope to welcome you home from your third trip to Vietnam. I want to personally thank you for years of service to our country. I wish that the cost of your service wasn't so high a price."
    Carol Pope (Camano Island, Washington)

"I read your tract, *The Most Powerful Verse*, several times and wanted to write and say, job well done. . . wonderful message."
    William Mitchell (Author / CEO P.O.P.S. International)

"I can't begin to tell you how much I enjoyed these can't put down books! Not only did I find myself eager to see what happens next, every time I did put them down my husband took them and started reading! I feel these powerful books should appeal to all, both young and old. They should be a source of hope and inspiration to every Vietnam vet and their family, every Christian and everyone on the journey to finding Christ. My only question is when does the next one come out?
    Sarah Green (Essexville, MI)

"I just finished your book and was really blessed by it. Your description of your ministry and God's faithfulness was a true encouragement, especially in the areas of God's leading and answered prayer.
    Pastor Bill Pratt (Immanuel Lutheran Church, St. Paul, MN)

"Your books are nearly impossible to put down. You have such a special personal way of writing, it speaks to the heart.
    Nancy Thomas (Cortey, Colorado)

"I do not have a lot of heroes I look up to, people that I say to myself, 'Now there is someone I wish I was more like.' But Den Slattery is one of those heroes."
    Larry May (Ravenna, MI)

"We really enjoyed *From the Point to the Cross*. You helped bring my husband Jim closer to the Lord."
    Martha Poolman (Kalamazoo, MI)

"I'm proud to say I know the author of *From the Point to the Cross*."
    Dr. Chuck Callahan (Colonel United States Army)

From the Point to the Cross is Great! So great that my husband and I want to order two more copies of it."
    Linda Smith (Dowagiac, MI)

Other Books by Den Slattery:
Life Goes On (1998)
Essential Truths (1997)
Essential Practices (2000)
Holding Christmas (Due out 2004)
Faith Talker (Due out 2004)

To Contact Den Slattery

den98@juno.com
or
denslattery@jackpine.com

**Point to the Cross Ministries, Inc.
3257 W. Kinney
Ludington, MI 48431**

Table Contents

INTRODUCTION	xiii
1. WHAT NOW?	1
2. 1967	3
3. M. C. R. D.	9
4. MARINE	13
5. VIETNAM	17
6. FIRE FIGHTS	21
7. I'M HIT	25
8. ROUTINE PATROLS	29
9. SADDLE UP	33
10. WALKING POINT	37
11. C. A. P.	41
12. GOING HOME	49
13. GETTING OUT	53
14. BACK TO NAM	59
15. WRESTLING WITH QUESTIONS	65
16. GETTING RIGHT	71
17. FOLLOW-UP	75
18. BAD HABITS	79
19. KOREA	83
20. POWER FOR LIVING	85
21. DELIVERANCE	91
22. WHAT REALLY HAPPENED?	97
23. GROWING IN GRACE	101
24. LED ASTRAY	105
25. IS ANYONE ALWAYS RIGHT?	109
26. BIBLE COLLEGE	113
27. HEARING GOD	117

28. YOUTH WITH A MISSION (Y.W.A.M.)	121
29. FAILURE	127
30. KAREN	131
31. GETTING IN	135
32. PASTOR DEN	139
33. KRISTIN	143
34. DARCY	147
35. ORDINATION	151
36. DAD	155
37. D.J.	161
38. TWO CHURCHES AT ONCE	165
39. JESUS WANTS YOU	169
40. IT NEVER HURTS TO ASK	173
41. SETTING THE CAPTIVE FREE	175
42. THE CROSS	181
43. THE LEADING OF GOD	187
44. YELLOW RIBBONS	193
EPILOGUE	197
RECOMMENDED BOOKS	199
DEN'S OTHER BOOKS	203

DEDICATION

This book is dedicated first and foremost to Jesus Christ.

Secondly, it is dedicated to my wife, Karen, who loves me as I am.

Thirdly, it is dedicated to my children (both natural and spiritual) in the hope that they can learn from the lessons in this book and not make the same mistakes I made.

INTRODUCTION

Everyone has a story and yet all of our stories are so different. Our stories help others know who we are and why we act the way we do. The story you are about to read is true. Some of the names have been changed to protect the innocent. However, the story remains factual. It spans a period of over thirty years and therefore only glimpses at key events that took me *From the Point to the Cross*. The "**Point**" in this story is a term used by the Marine Corps to describe the position of the man who walks in front of everyone else in an infantry unit. The "**Cross**" is the symbol worn by all Protestant Military Chaplains. Therefore, this is the story of how one pleasure seeking, atheistic, Marine pointman became a Protestant Military Chaplain.

This is not a "pie in the sky, everything is always wonderful" kind of book. It's about a real person with ups and downs, successes and failures, good days and bad days. I have made many mistakes in my life just like everyone else. Some of those mistakes you will read about in the pages that follow this introduction. I am not now, nor will I ever be in this life, a super-hero or perfect person. Yet in spite of my humanity, God has changed me through His Son, Jesus Christ, and used me in amazing ways. This is, therefore, the story of how such a change took place.

Any praise or glory that I may receive belongs to the Lord. For in a very real sense, this is His-story of what His grace and mercy can do to change the world one person at a time. This book is the story of how He changed me.

One of my favorite verses in the Bible expresses what I am attempting to say:

"But by the grace of God I am what I am, and His grace toward me was not in vain..." NKJV (I Corinthians 15:10)

My hope is that you will discover through this book that God is still in the life changing business. . . and I pray that He would change your life just as He has changed mine.

1

WHAT NOW?

"Well, Dennis, I think that's about all the questions we have for you now. Our committee needs some time to discuss our decision about whether or not to ordain you. We would ask that you wait in the lobby until we send someone for you. At that time we'll ask you to return to this room and we will inform you of our decision and why we made that decision. Do you have any questions?"

"No, I don't think so," I responded.

"All right, then, if you'll step out of the room, we'll let you know when we're ready for you."

As I walked out of that small conference room I felt a little apprehensive. The decision that this committee was about to make would determine my future vocation. My whole body felt tense as I paced back and forth in the lobby. This was about the fifteenth time I had been interviewed in the past six years. These interviews were part of the process for those desiring to be ordained to full-time ministry in the United Methodist Church. It had been a long journey that had led me to this final interview. I found myself reviewing all the key events in my mind as I waited.

I walked over to the large picture window and looked at the forest of trees surrounding the main lodge at Wesley Woods. It looked so peaceful outside in that forest, but as I looked at those trees I reflected back to a time when I was in a similar forest many years ago. In that forest I held a grenade in my hand ready to attack anyone who came near. I could almost feel the cold metal ball of steel in my hand as the trees in front of me changed to a dark and dangerous-looking forest on the other side of the world.

"Did you hear that?" John asked.
"Yeah, it sounded like something moving toward us." I responded.
John and I were Marines in Vietnam. We were fifty meters in front of our unit perimeter where 500 Marines waited to be attacked by Viet Cong and NVA soldiers. We held our weapons and grenades tightly as we watched for signs of movement in the dark forest in front of us. We had been hearing the sound of twigs breaking. Our hearts were beating so loudly that we thought the enemy could surely hear. The snapping twigs kept getting closer and closer. We knew the enemy was out there and we were ready to engage them. I took a grenade and pulled the pin with shaking hands. The noises grew louder and I thought I could detect the sound of voices in hushed tones. It was hard to see and hear in the forest at night. Shadows were everywhere.

John grabbed a grenade and pulled the pin. Sweat was dripping off my face and hands. The noises in front of us sounded like footsteps. We drew back our arms and on the count of three threw the grenades in the general direction of the noises. Several seconds later they exploded and lit up the dark forest.

I turned my head away from the window. The explosion brought me back to Wesley Woods. I walked away from the window to a chair by the fireplace. The memories were still too vivid. I sat down, but I was too tense to sit for long. I went back to the window and placed my hand on the adjoining wall. It was as if the window had become a looking glass into my past. How did I ever end up here applying to become a pastor? It had been a long journey, a journey that actually started in my senior year of high school.

2

<u>1967</u>

I was born on Good Friday in 1949 at Hackley Hospital, located in Muskegon, Michigan. I was the middle of three children and the only boy. Most of my growing up years were spent in Jackson, Michigan. However, we did spend a few of those years in Illinois and actually bought one of the first houses in Hoffman Estates – a now famous suburb of Chicago where one of the largest Churches in America exists, Willow Creek Community Church. But church was not something I was interested in during my early years. It seemed too boring and irrelevant. We went occasionally but we didn't let it interfere with how we lived our lives. We learned a few rote prayers but weren't really into reading the Bible or living anything close to a holy life. I just wanted to have fun and enjoy life while it lasted. And with that attitude, it's no wonder I didn't do very well in school. Even I was amazed when 1967 arrived and as a senior I had enough credits to graduate.

"What do you want to do after you graduate, Denny?" my friend Roger asked.

"I don't know yet."

How could someone 18 years old know what he wanted to do for the rest of his life? I sure didn't know. About the only thing I was sure of was that I wanted to be done with school. I never really loved school the way some kids did. For me it was something I had to endure but not something I necessarily enjoyed. There were times when my family and I wondered if I would ever graduate from high school. However, in June of 1967 I was proud to be walking down that hall with my cap and gown on along with the rest of my class. Our graduation ceremony was being held in the large dome-shaped gymnasium of Parkside High School located in Jackson, Michigan. I felt some remorse because I knew that my high school days were over and the future loomed in front of me as something dark and mysterious. I had no idea where I was going in life.

We marched to our seats as the school band played the song *Pomp and Circumstance*. It was a hot June day sitting there in our caps and gowns listening to speeches that no one really wanted to hear. Eventually, the speeches were over and the diplomas given out. When it was over I left that crowded gymnasium with the question that many of my classmates were probably also asking themselves, "What am I going to do now?"

There was one thing I knew I didn't want to do and that was to join the military. A lot of my friends were signing up because of the war in Vietnam, but not me. I knew I didn't want to go some place where people were trying to kill me. I enjoyed living too much for that. I also knew that I didn't want to go to college. My other options included bumming around the country, trying to find a job, or joining the Peace Corps. I decided to try getting a job.

That summer I worked part-time as a janitor for a large department store. I didn't like the work, but it kept me busy and gave me some spending money. One day the company had all of their several hundred employees take a test. I took it and apparently did fairly well. I was told to report to the main office for an interview about a new job working on computers - - in 1967 very few people knew much about computers. When I arrived for the interview there was an attractive young lady also chosen for the same job. They gave us a tour of their facilities and explained the computer position they were hoping to fill. Everyone was very positive and indicated that both of us showed potential. However, I found out later that they chose the attractive young lady instead of me just because they felt I would probably be drafted and sent to Vietnam. So I went back to being a janitor.

When summer was over I decided to look for a different kind of job with a better future. Since I had very few skills the possibilities were somewhat

1967

limited. Yet I did hear about an opportunity to be around some very wealthy people. I interviewed for the job and they hired me right away. It was true that I would be around some wealthy people but only to park their fancy cars. I would be working as a full-time parking lot attendant. To them I was a nobody. I parked their cars, collected their money, and while I waited for new customers, I did something I never thought I would do – I developed a love for reading. While in school I was never a very good reader and everything that our teachers asked us to read seemed boring. But when I could choose my own books, I became very interested. However, as the months rolled by, it soon began to dawn on me that I had discovered another job that I could add to my list of the things I wouldn't want to do for the rest of my life: be a parking lot attendant.

So I decided to try college, on a purely experimental basis, at least that's what the counselor told me it would be. I believe he called it "probation." I had graduated from high school in the bottom 10% of my class. My attitude hadn't been very good either so the college felt they were taking a chance on me. They tried to determine if I could do the work. I had no idea what courses to take so I just took what the counselor said would apply to almost any field of study: Political Science, Basic Math, Introduction to Psychology and English Composition. When the semester was over, I amazed everyone by passing _all_ my classes (Political Science was always borderline). With this new victory under my belt I signed up for another semester of courses.

However, as summer began, I received a letter in the mail that I was to undergo a complete physical examination for the draft board. This was for the express purpose of determining my draft classification. When the day arrived I reluctantly went.

That whole day was spent in long lines with hundreds of other guys, all wearing only our underwear and shoes. I felt like an animal in the zoo being herded around for inspection. The people who were performing the inspection treated us like we were criminals. I was inwardly hoping they would find something wrong with me so I could be forever free from their threats, but when the day was over, I was pronounced FIT FOR DUTY. If it hadn't been for my enrollment in college, I would have been drafted right away. When they were finished with us I was glad to be getting on the bus bound for home instead of boot camp.

From the Point to the Cross

That summer was great! The days and nights were filled with dates, parties and dancing. But when August arrived my whole attitude about life changed. The girl I was dating seemed too demanding, and I was beginning to feel like I should start seeing other girls. I wasn't looking forward to returning to college in the fall, and I was being hassled by my new alcoholic stepfather. Life seemed dull. I wanted to break out of the shell that was hemming me in, but I didn't know how.

Then one day Doug Eader, a friend of mine who had lived just across the street, came home for a visit after being gone for several years. Doug was about a year older than I was, but we had been friends during our high school days.

He was dressed in his Army uniform with medals and awards all neatly displayed. He had just returned from Vietnam where he had served for the past twelve months with the 101st Airborne Division.

"What was it like over there?" I asked as a group of my friends gathered around Doug to listen.

"Well," Doug began, "Vietnam is different from anywhere else in the world. It's mostly made up of rice paddies and jungles, and it's hotter than any place I've ever been. It has bugs I never even knew existed and, man, are they big!"

"Tell us about the war, Doug," someone said.

"Yeah, is it just like they show on TV?" my sister asked.

Doug looked down for a moment and shook his head slowly. "No, it's not like they show you on TV. Those reporters seem to twist things around to fit in with their own biases. I've read of battles that I've been in and after the media was done with them they made them sound like totally different battles. The reporters just don't get the facts straight."

Doug paused and looked as if he were back in the jungles of Vietnam for a moment and then he said in a voice that sounded far away, "It's a terrible war and a lot of innocent people are being killed."

Just then someone asked the one question that always comes up when talking about war, "Have you killed anyone?"

Doug looked at the person who asked the question and without a moment's hesitation said, "Yes, I have. I've killed a lot of people."

1967

No one said a word for a moment until Doug broke the silence, "It's not like you think. In Vietnam we became like hunted animals. We didn't see the 'gooks' as people but as animals that walk on two legs instead of four. They were animals that had killed our buddies and murdered women and children. Fighting people like that made us become hardened. The enemy is not like a civilized person. They're like hungry tigers that are looking for their next meal."

"Did you ever torture anyone?" someone asked.

"Yeah, a few times we did. Usually we'd get in a helicopter and go up a thousand feet or so and then start asking questions through an interpreter. If we didn't get the response we were looking for we'd throw one of them out of the chopper. It's amazing what a little persuasion will do. Some of the guys would even cut off the ears of gooks and make a belt or necklace out of them. The only problem was it drew a lot of flies. And, man, does Vietnam have the flies!"

Doug went on telling his amazing story which sounded kind of hard to believe, even though he swore it was all true. He also told us all about his medals for bravery, and about the three Purple Hearts he received for not ducking at the right time.

It was because of the adventure element in his story that I went to visit the Marine recruiter the very next day. I had always heard that the Marine Corps was the toughest branch of the military and that they were always on the lookout for a few good men. I figured that if I was going to end up in Vietnam I wanted to go with the best. I signed up and two weeks later boarded a jet for California. I was headed for basic training as a Marine. I was ready for my life of adventure to begin.

3

M. C. R. D.

As the plane soared into the blue sky on that warm August day, I had visions of returning home some day as a hero with my own war stories and decorated uniform. I sat back in the seat and tried to enjoy the flight.

The sun was just setting as we landed in California. I had often thought of visiting California with its movie stars, beaches and beautiful girls. However, my dream vacation didn't include the Marine Corps.

Those of us who had been sworn in as Marines back in Detroit were instructed to stay together. We wandered around the airport like we were in a new country. Eventually, we were greeted by some Marines in uniform and loaded onto a military bus. Our new home for the next fifteen weeks would be the Marine Corps Recruiting Depot (M.C.R.D.) located in San Diego. As we drove through the front gates, I noticed the strange igloo-shaped Quonset huts. The bus moved slowly through the narrow streets of the post until it finally came to a stop in back of some old buildings that looked like warehouses.

The door to the bus opened and in stepped a big, mean looking Marine wearing the traditional Smoky the Bear hat.

"I'm your new Drill Instructor (DI). What that means is that I'm like God to you people. I'll tell you when to speak, when to eat, when to move, when to smoke, and even when you can take a trip to the John. If I don't tell you to do something, you don't do it. You got that?"

The DI began walking toward the rear of the bus but then came to an abrupt stop in front of one young man sitting on the edge of his seat and partially blocking the aisle.

"What are you smiling at?" the DI asked the young man. Then without any warning the DI slapped that new recruit in the head so hard that he fell on the floor, into the aisle of the bus.

"Get up!" the DI demanded.

Then turning his eyes from the aisle to the rest of us, he said, "I'm giving you GIRLS ten seconds to grab your gear and get off this bus. When I say 'move' I want you to go and stand on those footprints by the building. Now MOVE!"

The DI quickly got off the bus while the rest of us scrambled for our gear and then the door. The last man off the bus was kicked and told to drop for push-ups. The rest of us had to stand on the footprints while the DI paced back and forth looking us over. Several minutes later he stood in front of the group and began his introductory speech.

"You PUKES are a wretched sight. To think that the Corps is going to waste its money on you by trying to turn you into fighting Marines is hard to believe. I want to know right off if any of you long haired freaks are queer or female. If you're either one of those, you don't belong in MY Marine Corps."

The DI moved toward one of the new recruits with long hair.

"How about you, you long haired freak. Are you a queer?"

"No way, man, not me," the young man responded.

The DI quickly jabbed him in the stomach. As the young man folded his arms around his stomach, the DI leaned over him and said, "You call me SIR, boy. You got that?"

"Yes, sir."

"Boy, the first and last words out of your mouth are to be 'sir.'"

"Sir, yes, sir."

"Now what about it, boy, are you a queer?"

"Sir, no, sir!"

The DI backed away from the boy knowing that he had established his authority. When he was in front of the group he began his speech again.

M. C. R. D.

"Now it's time to give you freaks a haircut. Our barbers have been given strict orders to give you the latest style, whether you want it or not. We call it the Marine Corps recruit style. Now when I say move, I want you to run to that building over there and stand in line until it's your turn to go in. You got that?"

"Sir, yes, sir," we all quickly responded.

"MOVE OUT!"

We ran for the building not wanting to be the last person to arrive. It was every man for himself. While in line we had to stand so close to each other that there was barely room to turn our heads. We soon discovered that our special haircut was a scalp job. The barbers really seemed to enjoy their work, especially when one of the guys with long hair sat down.

With our new haircuts we were hustled into another room where we had to stand in a long line to receive our clothing. Even those giving out the clothes seemed to treat us like we were criminals. Once we had a bag full of new military clothing we were ushered into a different room where we had to sit on the floor and wait for everyone else to finish. The DI then told us we couldn't wear HIS clothes until we had a shower. There was a little moaning at his suggestion so he had us take off all our clothes and squeeze into a large shower room, where we were instructed to get on the floor. Once everyone was in place he turned the cold water on and made us lay there and sing the Marine Corps Hymn. Most of us didn't even know the Marine Corps Hymn, but we tried to learn it real fast. With our shower completed we were allowed to put on our new uniforms.

Next, the DI told us to stand at attention in a room with a lot of tables. One of the recruits passed out and hit his head on a heating register. The DI went over to him and kicked him in the side and called him a sissy. It was obvious that he was not a man of compassion. We were told to take everything we brought with us and put it into boxes, which would be sent home with a brief note to "mommy" saying that we had arrived safely.

We weren't allowed any sleep that first night. We were humiliated and degraded in every way possible. We quickly discovered that in the Marine Corps everything must be done in a hurry, whether it was the five minutes they allowed us to eat our meals or the two minutes they allowed us in the bathroom (head).

After several days we were put in permanent Platoons and given Quonset huts to sleep in. It was at this point that our lives began to take on some regularity. Our day usually began about 4:00 AM with exercise and a morning run. At 5:00 AM we would eat breakfast and then return to our huts to shower, shave, and clean our areas. At 6:00 AM we went to classes which continued throughout the day and into the night. All new recruits were kept on edge not just by the training but because of the constant harassment. One day we had to walk like ducks for several hundred yards because we didn't march well. Our days were filled with such episodes of harassment. It's all part of the being in the Marines.

On one of our first long runs many of the men were falling out, so I decided to do the same. However, the DI had other plans. He came up from behind and hit me in the back of the head so hard that he knocked me to the ground. He then kicked me and told me to get up. When I did, he hit me in the head again causing me to lose my balance and fall back on the ground. Eventually, he allowed me to get back in the formation and complete the run. Those who didn't finish had to go out and do it again or face going to the "PIG FARM" or "MOTIVATION" - - places for those who either couldn't or wouldn't do the exercises.

As the days passed, I somehow kept hoping that I would wake up and find out this had all been just a bad dream. But it finally dawned on me that this was not a nightmare but reality. I couldn't comprehend how there could be such a place as this in the civilized world. I felt like an animal. Somehow my dreams of adventure seemed far away as they forced us each night to sing the Marine Corps Hymn and to say good night to the greatest Marine of all time,

"Good night, Chesty Puller, wherever you are."

4

MARINE

    Boot camp was tough. There were moments when I didn't think I would ever get out of that first phase of my training. I learned an important lesson during those difficult days: disciplined endurance. I learned how to go on even when I felt like I couldn't go any further. My body would be tired, but if I determined in my mind to go on, I could do it.

    It took thirteen weeks to complete Marine Corps Boot Camp. On the final day we had a large graduation ceremony on the parade field. Since graduation was the goal of our training, they made a big deal of it. After all the parades, ceremonies, and speeches, we were allowed our first freedom since arriving. Most of us walked around in our dress uniforms and over-indulged in junk food, which we had been denied for the full thirteen weeks of training.

    We were now called "Marine" instead of "Slime". Therefore, we felt confident that things would be different for us once we got to our new training site. But when we arrived at Camp Pendleton we once again felt like new recruits fresh off the bus.

    "OK, you Marines get off that bus NOW!"

    Those words were spoken by a Buck Sergeant in a Smoky the Bear hat while he stood at the door of our bus. We all scrambled for our gear and got off that bus just as fast as we could.

From the Point to the Cross

"Fall in behind a footlocker!" the sergeant said, pointing toward a long row of footlockers.

Once everyone was in place we were instructed to grab our gear and the footlocker and double-time (run) to a building about 200 yards away.

"Now, move out, Marines!"

The Marine Corps had decided that I would make a good infantryman, so they sent me to a six week advanced infantryman training school. In addition to the class work, the training was every bit as hard physically as boot camp. We learned to route-step (walk out of step but in formation). This was done at a very fast pace so that some people had to run to keep up. I never knew there were so many hills in California.

At one point in our training they asked for the really gun-ho Marines to volunteer for "Forced Recon." Their task was to go in behind enemy lines in small three to five man units and gather information about the enemy. I was pressured to be in that group, but when I discovered that I would have to jump out of perfectly good planes, usually in the middle of the night, I backed away. Every other aspect of the program sounded interesting, but there was no way I was going to volunteer to parachute thousands of feet in the air into pitch darkness. I was looking for adventure, but even I had my limits.

At the end of our training we received our orders for our next duty assignment. My orders said I was to report back to Camp Pendleton for Advanced Jungle Training. After the jungle training I would be sent to Vietnam. Somehow just seeing the word Vietnam on my orders jolted me. I realized that soon I would be seeing that strange place that my friend, Doug, had described to me. It didn't seem quite as glorious now that I knew I would be going there.

However, I noticed that my orders also said I would be allowed to have 30 days leave before I had to report back to Camp Pendleton. Since it was almost Christmas that meant I would be able to be home for the holidays. That was something to be excited about.

I felt good. I had gained about twenty pounds of muscle from all the PT (Physical Training) they made us do and I was proud to be wearing my Marine uniform.

Marine

As my family greeted me at the airport in Detroit, they remarked on how much stronger I looked. They had all kinds of questions to ask me about my training as we drove toward home.

When we arrived, I quickly changed clothes and then rushed over to my old girlfriend's house. She seemed to be excited about seeing me but also revealed, in the course of our conversation, that she had been dating someone else. In spite of that fact, she kept telling me that she really loved me. For some reason I had a hard time believing her. We were drifting apart and there was nothing I could do to change it. We dated during my thirty days leave, but when we said good-bye, I knew it was good-bye forever.

I reported in for Jungle Training at Camp Pendleton, California. It was there that I learned how to hunt small game and how to survive off the land. During one 24-hour period we were P.O.W.'s in a simulated Vietnamese prison camp. When our three-week jungle school was over, we packed our duffle bags and prepared for our next destination: Vietnam.

When the day of our departure arrived I was surprised to see that we would be flying on regular commercial planes. The comfort helped to make the trip more bearable. We landed in Okinawa and for some reason ended up staying there for almost a month. Okinawa was great compared to what we expected to find in Vietnam.

However, the word eventually came down through channels that they were ready for us now. Therefore, we boarded the plane heading for Vietnam. All of us were much quieter now than during the first part of the trip. There was an attitude of seriousness as we wondered if we would live to make the return trip home in twelve months

It was a short flight from Okinawa to Vietnam. After a quick snack the stewardess interrupted us:

"Could I please have your attention for a moment? We are only a few minutes away from the border of South Vietnam. As all of you know, Vietnam is a hostile land. There is a good chance that we may be fired upon, so we are flying in late at night and flying very high. When we near the airport we will be making our descent very rapidly. We would ask that you keep your seat belt on and that you gather your belongings together NOW so that you won't have to look for them later. We would also ask that you deplane as quickly as possible once we are on the ground. Thank you."

From the Point to the Cross

    This announcement made all of us tense, but we did as we were asked and then waited in silence. It wasn't long before we felt our plane do something of a nose-dive over the airport. Several minutes later we felt the wheels touch pavement. We were in Vietnam.

5

VIETNAM

    Our plane landed at the DaNang airport in South Vietnam at about 3:00 AM. It was dark outside and the air terminal was hard to make out due to poor lighting. When the plane rolled to a stop, the doors swung open and Marines started hustling out as fast as they could.
    When I finally stuck my head out the door of the plane the air was so hot and heavy that it took my breath away for a moment. I stumbled down the steps and hurried after the others who were running for the bunkers. I kept thinking that we were going to be shot and killed just getting off the plane. As I ran for the bunker, I reflected back on the DI who told us to get off the bus in a hurry. Now I realized the importance of it. When we arrived at the bunkers we dropped our gear and sat down to await further orders. Soon the sun was peeking over the mountains that surrounded DaNang and we still had no further orders. How typical of the military to make you hurry to one spot and then sit around for hours waiting for further direction. We call this the "Hurry Up and Wait" principle.
    By mid-morning the air terminal was flooded with people. At one point I noticed a 3/4-ton truck pull up with three men in it. One man was driving and the other two were standing behind the cab of the truck holding onto an M-60 machine gun. They all looked so much like the John Wayne type that I had to look again. Their uniforms were faded and their boots had no visible polish. They had machine gun ammunition strung over their shoulders in

Mexican crisscross fashion and they had holsters strapped on their sides. As a new recruit I was very impressed. I envisioned myself looking just like them, when in reality I looked so clean and neat that I belonged more in a stateside marching band."Maybe someday I'll look like them," I thought.

At about noon a truck arrived to take us to our new unit: Third Battalion Seventh Marines. We were headed for a base camp just outside DaNang. The base camp was located on the outside edge of the rocket belt; the farthest distance that an enemy rocket could be fired and still hit DaNang. The job of the Third Battalion Seventh Marines (3/7) was to patrol the rocket belt and try to stop "Charlie" from shooting rockets at the American bases in DaNang.

We boarded our truck and headed for the 3/7 base camp. The air felt good as we drove along the dirt roads. ZING! "Get down!" someone shouted, "We're being shot at!" We all got as close to the deck of that truck as we could and the driver began to drive like a wild man. ZING, ZING, ZING. I discovered later that sometimes when new recruits arrive the old timers play tricks on them like making them think they are being shot at when they aren't. We were shot at several more times before we finally arrived at our base camp, without any casualties, of course. We unloaded the trucks and were assigned a hooch (tin shack) and a bunk. The rest of the day was ours to get settled. I squared away my gear and then stretched out on my new bunk and went to sleep.

When I woke up it was dark outside and there were loud explosions and people screaming, "INCOMING!" While this word was not currently a part of my everyday vocabulary, I quickly surmised that it meant we were being attacked. There was so much confusion with people running in every direction that I didn't know what to do. They hadn't even given us a weapon yet and now we were under enemy attack. I felt helpless.

However, it seemed to me that I'd stand a better chance if I was not inside a building so I went outside. I stood in the dark and just waited for a few seconds to get my bearings. Noticing a bunker about forty yards from my position, I ran for it. When I reached the bunker I found several other Marines hiding there too. What a relief to be with other Marines. I realized then that Marines were not invincible, yet it was comforting to be together while under attack. We watched the show from our bunker. Red and green tracers were lighting up the night in an effort to pinpoint where the rounds were landing. The 105's and the 155's were firing their heavy artillery rounds as if to warn those on the receiving end to come no further but to retreat. Just then we heard a plane coming in overhead, followed by a loud humming noise and a constant stream of red tracers being hurled at the earth below.

"That's Puff the Magic Dragon," one Marine said. "He can cover a whole football field in one pass and put one round in every square foot of it."

I was impressed. It seemed that the battle ended almost as soon as "Puff" came on the scene. The rest of the night was quiet. We all returned to our hooch's and tried to get back to sleep.

When morning arrived someone ordered that a body count be taken. Body counts were the only way we could tell if we were effective in our efforts during the Vietnam War. Since we were not permitted to do anything to win, as in other wars, we used body counts to tell us who was winning the war. No Marines were hurt that night but several Viet Cong had been killed. It was often hard to get an accurate count since the bodies were torn in pieces by the heavy artillery rounds or dragged off by their comrades.

For those of us who were new to the unit, our day began with a grand tour of the base. I was surprised at how nonchalant everyone was about the attack the previous night. Some of the men even seemed to enjoy it. They laughed at us and called us names like "Boot", "Mr. Clean", "Cherry" and, their favorite, "Newbee." How tough you were seemed to be determined by how long you had been in Vietnam and still lived to tell about it. The guys that had been there the longest were called "Short", a term which meant that they were close to going home. The normal tour of duty for Marines was thirteen months, if you lived that long.

6

FIRE FIGHTS

    The orientation to our base lasted about five days. When it was over we were assigned to various sized companies, ranging anywhere from 30 to 60 men, and allowed to begin doing our jobs. The time had finally arrived for me to go on my first patrol and actually take an active role in this war. It would be a squad-sized patrol of sixteen men. I met with my squad, and we received ammunition, grenades and flares. Then we all stood around until the squad leader and platoon sergeant (SGT) came over with last minute instructions. They laid a map on the table with some red and black markings on it.
    "This is where we are now, and this is your first check point. It will also be where you will set up your first ambush for the evening," he said as he pointed to a spot not far from our base camp. "Your other two check points are each two kilometers (clicks) apart. At about midnight you move out to check point three to set up your second ambush. Any questions?"
    With that the Sergeant was gone and we were told to saddle up. Once we all had our gear on we began our patrol. I felt proud to be going on a patrol, although I wasn't sure what to expect. There was a sense of apprehension among the men. There would always be the question in the back of our minds, "What will happen out there tonight?" However, at that moment an even more important question was racing through my mind, "Will I make it back alive or is this it for me?" It only takes one bullet or one explosion

to totally alter your life or possibly end it. Eventually, I would learn to live with that fear.

We all lined up on opposite sides of the road leading away from the base camp. We staggered our positions so that at least ten meters separated each man, for if we walked too close to each other one rocket or a grenade could take all of us out.

The sun was just going down as we approached the nearby village. We walked slowly past the small hooch's (shacks) where the people lived. We had all heard stories of how the Viet Cong lived in villages in the daytime and at night would sneak out for their terrorist activities. Most of them didn't wear uniforms so we never knew who to trust and who not to trust. Even the women and children were often used by the enemy.

Children would often approach a group of soldiers asking for candy, which we were more than happy to supply. They were so cute and friendly that we couldn't turn them away. But the Viet Cong knew that Americans loved little children so they would attach explosive devices under the children's clothes and then send them into a group of soldiers. When the soldiers were close enough to the children the Viet Cong would detonate the explosives, thus killing the children and the soldiers. We never got used to that kind of reasoning. Most of the children were just innocent victims of the war who were thrown into harms way. However, if they approached us with weapons or explosives we had no choice but to shoot them. Yet the American soldiers I knew who had to shoot children never forgot it and often had nightmares about it years later.

As we reached the outskirts of town our patrol stopped. The squad leader disappeared and then returned several minutes later. When the patrol moved out again we went in the direction the squad leader had gone. We all hurried into a type of old fort surrounded by a barbed wire fence. There was a tall lookout tower at the far end of the camp with a .50 caliber machine gun. Sandbags were strung out in every direction. I also noticed a trench that was apparently used to defend the fort.

Once we were in the trench the squad leader told us we were going to "sandbag" (not go out) on our normal patrol. Instead we were going to stay with this Combined Action Group (CAG) unit. I had no idea that one day I would be a part of a CAG team. The night passed without any enemy contact.

Fire Fights

When the sun broke over the horizon we returned to our base camp. I was glad to be returning but didn't feel very proud of what we had done. I kept thinking that someone would find out and tell the Captain and then we'd all be in hot water. Since nothing ever did happen, I assumed that meant he never found out, or if he did he just didn't care.

I discovered that each squad only had to go out on patrol about every third or fourth night. The rest of the time we had to man the bunkers or be involved in working parties. The working party I was put on after that first patrol was to clean the port-a-Johns. We basically just threw diesel fuel on the mess and set it on fire. I hated that job and had lots of exposure to it to know just how much I hated it.

On the nights we didn't have guard duty or a patrol, most of us could be found in the club drinking pop or beer (when available) and watching a movie. Once in a while, the USO would send a band with girls who would dance and sing. I went to the club every night that I wasn't busy with the war. Yet that third night would always arrive and I would have to go back out on patrol.

I had been in Vietnam for about a month and still had not been in a firefight with the enemy while on a patrol. We heard of other patrols getting hit, but not my squad. I had no way of knowing that things were about to change.

One night we went to our first ambush site for the evening and set up just as the darkness of the night enveloped us. A few minutes later we were under attack. Tracers began flying in every direction.

Someone yelled, "GET DOWN . . .GET DOWN . . .WE'RE GETTING HIT!"

At that moment I was lying behind a rice paddy dike that only stood about eighteen inches high. Bullets were flying all around me. They were so close that I could hear them whiz by my ear. I looked down at my feet and saw tracers hitting on both sides of me but somehow missing their mark. I tried to raise my rifle to fire but found I couldn't fire due to the steady stream of bullets coming my way. I felt helpless and scared. It wasn't anything like the John Wayne movies.

In that moment of shear terror I saw my life race before me as if it were my final reflection before the end. I had never really known this kind of fear before. Somehow all the glory of war faded into the distance as I heard men screaming in the dark and crying for help. I suddenly realized in that moment that I wasn't ready to die.

While I was lying there in that rice paddy awaiting my own death, questions began to form in my mind that would haunt me for years to come:

Why am I here?
Is this all there is to life?
What is the purpose of life?
Is there a God?
What happens when we die?

I didn't have any idea how to deal with those questions. I was a tough Marine and we didn't talk about philosophy or religion. But I determined then and there that if I lived through that night, I would search for the answers to those questions.

Just then the shooting stopped. It was over and I was still alive. I never even fired a shot in my first firefight. The rest of the night passed without incident, and when the sun rose we headed for our base camp feeling very fortunate just to be alive to see another day.

7

I'M HIT

The next day I was put on another working party. It was an exceptionally hot day and we were assigned the task of clearing some bushes and small trees. Everyone just wanted to be done with it so we could get out of the sun. I was over working on a small tree trying to chop it down when suddenly there was an explosion. Dirt was flying everywhere and people were screaming. I found myself on the ground several feet from where I had been. There was a stinging feeling on my face and my arms. My eyes felt like they were on fire. I couldn't see anything. I cried out for help and tried to stumble to my feet.

"I'm hit! I can't see! Help me! I can't see!"

Someone grabbed me and with the help of others eventually took me to the base dispensary. Upon our arrival several people rushed me to an examination table. They laid me down and rinsed my eyes out with water over and over again. Someone grabbed my arm and used what felt like a wire brush on my wounds, sending increased pain throughout my already painful body. Someone else leaned over and said they were sending for a helicopter to get me to a hospital where they could treat me for the wounds I had received.

"Am I gonna be OK?" I asked.

"It's hard to say at this point, but your wounds don't look too deep so you should be OK," replied the person speaking.

From the Point to the Cross

When the chopper arrived I was loaded on board. I had a patch on one eye, but I could see a little out of the other eye.

With my good eye I was able to see another person on board who had lost a leg. I was a little relieved that I couldn't see clearly enough to get a good look at him or his exposed leg. It felt good to be flying away from the war to safety. I sat back and tried to enjoy the ride in spite of the pain and uncertainty of my condition.

Much to my surprise we landed on a ship a short distance from the shore. People scrambled over to us and helped us get off the chopper. As they escorted us back to the hospital section I overheard someone say, "Not much this time. Just a leg wound and some guy with shrapnel in one eye. Maybe next time we'll get some good ones."

"Oh well," I thought, "I'm kinda glad it's nothing too serious."

Small pieces of metal and dirt were taken out of my arm and my eye was cleaned several times. After an extensive exam, a doctor gave me his analysis.

"You're a lucky man, Mr. Slattery. Those wounds didn't get much below the skin. Your eye will be sore for a few days but with regular rinsing and a few days to recover you should be back in your unit in about a week."

He was right.

However, after hospital life with beautiful American nurses, good food and safety, I wasn't too excited about returning to the life of a combat infantryman. Yet within a week I was released from the hospital and sent back to my unit. A few days after my return I was sent back out on patrol. I was a little leery, but orders are orders.

I'll never forget that first night out again. It started off like any normal patrol, but it didn't end that way. As on previous patrols, we had to go through a series of check-points and then set up an ambush in two different locations. We arrived at our first ambush site at about 10:00 PM. We spread out, found some cover, and then figured out our fields of fire. The mosquitoes were terrible. Two hours went by and no sign of any enemy movement in the area. So at midnight we moved to our second ambush site.

Once we arrived at our second site, I got into position with the three other members of my fire team. As I scanned the horizon around us I thought I saw some movement on a small hill. It moved again. And then again. The silhouette looked like a man, so I told the other members of my fire team. Silently we all watched. There it was again. We sent word to the

I'm Hit

sergeant and moments later we were told to open fire. We took aim and then our "Blooperman" with the M-79 grenade launcher let one fly.

As soon as his round hit we all opened fire. The next few minutes were filled with the sounds of war and people screaming. Red tracers and explosions were lighting up the darkness around us. Then our sergeant yelled, "Cease fire! Cease fire!" The night was suddenly silent.

Eventually, the word trickled back to us that we had shot our own men. One of the other squads from our platoon had decided to "sandbag" their second ambush site. We killed three and wounded two others. That would not be the last time such a mistake would be made. As a matter of fact, I would discover later that this type of incident would be repeated hundreds of times over the course of the war. They were casualties of the war. Accidents. Very costly, tragic mistakes. Those mistakes heightened our fear that if the enemy didn't get us, friendly fire might.

When the sun broke over the horizon that next morning we all stumbled back to our base camp with our heads hanging low. Not much was said about the incident except a reminder that no one should sandbag patrols again. Several days later we went back out on patrol as if nothing had happened. The war must go on.

8

ROUTINE PATROLS

    The days seemed to drag by. My mental attitude was extremely bleak as I fought the intense heat and the war itself. There were always more patrols and people getting hurt. I tried not to get very close to the other men in my unit, just as a way of shielding myself from the sorrow of losing a good friend. I figured, why even try to become close friends with men who could be the next one to be wounded, maimed or killed? But it was impossible not to feel bonded to men who were willing to put their lives on the line for me.

    To make matters worse, my girlfriend from back home sent me what we called a "Dear John" letter, even though my name wasn't John. She wanted her freedom to date other men. We both knew there was no guarantee that I would ever make it back alive. I tried to conceal my hurt from the other guys, but the letter devastated me, even though I expected it. What made matters worse was that there wasn't anything I could do about it. I couldn't even call her and try to talk it out. So I just sat there on my bunk reading the letter over and over. As I read I thought about the things we had done together and the plans we had for the future. Now it was all being washed down the drain. Yes I had expected it, and yet inwardly I had hoped it wouldn't happen. In my last letter to her I had tried to push her to be honest with me about our future together. Now I had my answer.

Just then my squad leader came in and yelled from the door, "Saddle up. We have a routine patrol to go on. Get your gear and meet me in five minutes by the bulletin board." With that he was gone.

We put our letters and books away, and then grabbed our weapons and gear as we headed out the door. Gathering by the bulletin board, it soon became apparent that we were going on a daytime mission with the whole company. We went through the normal routine of getting our general game plan, stocking up on ammo, making sure everyone was there, and finally loading our weapons. We were to go to a designated area in search of enemy locations and then meet up with the rest of our company. Our assigned area was just outside the local village.

My squad had to walk across many dried up rice paddies. When we were only about 100 meters from our destination, suddenly there was an explosion. Our natural reaction was to hit the ground, look for cover and try to locate the enemy, all in the flash of a second. As the smoke cleared someone crawled to the point man who was groaning in pain.

"Corpsman up!"

The corpsman crawled to the wounded man and I could hear the radioman calling in a medivac helicopter. We formed a semi-perimeter to secure the area and waited. The point man had stepped on some type of booby trap that had just blown off both of his legs and caused other wounds as well. We all sat and listened as he asked about his legs and then heard him cry as he discovered they were gone. This was a fate worse than death, or so most of us thought. One minute you're up walking around, and a split second later your legs are gone.

The chopper arrived within ten minutes of the call. Before it even touched down the crew chief was off and heading for the wounded man. They quickly loaded him on the helicopter and then lifted off the ground, leaving us in a cloud of dust.

"Smith, you and your fire team are the point team. Get us out of here," said the platoon sergeant. Smith was my fire team leader. For the next several months we would be the point (first) team, leading the way for everyone else. All of us were glad to get out of that area because there was a good chance that there were more surprises just waiting for someone to stumble upon. We moved out fast and were soon with the other elements of our company.

Routine Patrols

We were just in time to participate in a sweep of a wooded area about 300 meters to our south. Everyone got on line and used all the firepower we had before we took one step in that direction. My weapon jammed in the process and I couldn't fire. I swore at it as I began taking it apart. A lot of us didn't like the M-16 because it had a tendency to jam at any time. More than once it happened to me right in the middle of a firefight.

"Cease fire! Cease fire!" the captain commanded. "Let's move out SLOWLY. And stay on line."

When we got to the wooded area there was no sign of life. We did find a few tunnels with some weapons but nothing like what we anticipated. After searching the area thoroughly we headed back to our base camp. Most of us were just glad it was over so we could get back to the club to drown out the memories of this place in 3-2 Beer.

9

SADDLE UP

In the days that followed we began to hear rumors of an upcoming operation. Within the week our Company Commander confirmed it. Intelligence reports said that the NVA (North Vietnamese Army) were moving a lot of supplies into the area and that someone had to go and try to stop them. We were selected.

It was estimated that there were almost 3,000 enemy soldiers operating in that area. Therefore, higher headquarters decided to send in one Battalion of Marines (750 men). This was typical of Marine Corps strategy. The plan involved driving us to the base of the mountain range where we would begin our ascent into enemy territory. We were scheduled to leave in 48 hours.

Those 48 hours were filled with preparations. Weapons had to be cleaned, extra ammo drawn, backpacks filled, and PX (Post Exchange) runs made. We bought extra candy and other snacks to take with us. My pack was filled with shaving gear, letter writing materials, one change of clothes, snacks and C-Rations (3 meals). I also carried four hand grenades, four trip flares, four pop flares, one claymore mine, 100 rounds of machine gun ammo, my M-16 rifle, 25 magazines filled with ammunition, a poncho and poncho liner, three canteens of water, a first aid pack, an entrenching tool, bug repellent, water tablets, heat tabs for our food, and a knife. Each man was carrying between 50 and 120 pounds of extra weight.

From the Point to the Cross

We took off early in the morning and assembled in an area just below the mountains. Once we arrived we had to wait until everyone else was on the scene. After an hour or so, someone began singing the song "I Wanna Go Home" and it caught on until all of the battalion seemed to be singing together. Here we were thousands of miles from home, fighting someone else's war in a foreign land, and none of us really knew why we were there. Any of us would have jumped at the chance to go home but instead we had to stay and fight.

Back in America a lot of young people were protesting our being in Vietnam. We heard reports of demonstrations and riots, all in the name of peace. Our whole country seemed to be heading in the direction of a revolution. College students acted like they hated the American government system and all of its branches. Many people were calling those of us in Vietnam "baby killers" and "drug addicts." Even though most of us joined the military because we thought it was the noble thing to do when our country needed us, now we weren't so sure. It was hard to keep our patriotic ideals in the light of everything that was happening. Therefore, what many of us did was fought for our own survival because that was one thing we knew we believed in.

"Saddle up!" the commander ordered. We got to our feet and gathered up our gear. Several minutes later we began our journey up the mountain in front of us.

The first three days were easy. The mountains were cooler than the lowlands and we had no contact with the enemy. About once a day a helicopter flew into our position to drop off supplies and mail, both of which seemed vital for our existence. On the fourth and fifth days we ran into some small sniper fire, which slowed us down for several hours. We had to call in a medivac helicopter for the wounded and then search in vain for the sniper. We rarely found snipers. They were masters at camouflage. But they always seemed to find us and their constant harassment unsettled everyone. It was a type of psychological warfare.

By the seventh day we were wondering if the NVA were even in the area at all. My platoon was in the middle of a long line of soldiers strung out in an overgrown mountain forest. Suddenly without warning we heard that first crack of an AK-47 rifle. We hit the ground, found something to hide behind and waited. Within seconds there was the sound of automatic weapons, explosions, small arms fire, and men screaming.

Saddle Up

Our front platoon was under attack. My platoon just waited and listened. We kept wondering what was going on and if we too would soon be attacked. In fifteen minutes all was silent. Ten minutes later we got word to move out. It took us awhile to get to the place where the firefight actually took place. Fifteen of our men were wounded and three killed. We had to walk by our wounded friends to get to our position for the night. As we kept walking we passed by several Vietnamese who were riddled with bullet holes and covered in their own blood. They would not be buried but left for the enemy to see. We would set up a perimeter for the night and try to get some helicopters in for the wounded first thing in the morning.

The night was a quiet one. When the first light of dawn came, the helicopters arrived. As the first one touched down we began taking enemy fire. The wounded were loaded on board as the rest of us opened fire on the enemy. Seconds later the chopper was off and in the clear. The other chopper never did land. Now we had to move out carrying three dead men in body bags. We walked a long distance that day and those bodies became very heavy. Just as the sun was going down we reached a clearing where the choppers met us and we were able to evacuate the dead.

We were at the top of a mountainous region, which would become our new temporary base. We set up a perimeter for the night and dug our foxholes. We also put out trip flares and claymore mines in front of our positions, just in case we had visitors. We hated the nights in Vietnam. As the sunset we paired off and decided who would take the first watch. Someone had to be awake all night long because that was usually when the enemy attacked. The average infantryman would get about four hours of sleep a night in the bush.

Early the next morning I turned on my transistor radio just in time to hear the disc jockey say, "Gooooood morrrrrrrning, Vietnam." I had made it through another night.

10

WALKING POINT

Walking point had some real advantages. I always knew what was going on while those further back often had no idea. Being the pointman placed me where the action was. If anything was going to happen it usually happened toward the front of the patrol. As pointman I was at times allowed the freedom to make the decision as to which path to take. Sometimes that meant forging a trail with a machete through thick brush or high elephant grass. Being on point, I was encouraged to follow my gut feelings. I knew that if I made a mistake and missed something that I should have seen, it very easily could cost my own life or the lives of the other men following me.

By walking point I discovered the signals of danger. I watched and listened to the birds and animals and I paid close attention to the ground for signs of a booby trap. I often looked at the trees and bushes for any sign of an attacker in hiding. It was a very stressful and dangerous job. All of my senses worked overtime while I was out on point. I developed an acute sense of danger. Sights, sounds, smell, gut feelings, intuition and paying attention to the environment meant the difference between life and death. The life expectancy of a pointman in a Marine infantry unit during the Vietnam War was thought of in terms of how many minutes he survived in enemy territory. I was told that the average was about three minutes. I wanted to prove them wrong.

From the Point to the Cross

    I usually liked walking point even though I was afraid most of the time. More than an enemy bullet, I feared the booby traps that were a constant threat to my legs and future sex life. By some divine miracle, I walked the point man position for three months and never stepped on a booby trap or led my fellow Marines into an ambush. Other men in my unit weren't as fortunate since pointmen were constantly being wounded or killed.

    However, there was one event that happened while I was a pointman that I will never forget. It happened early one morning as my platoon was getting ready to go out on patrol. It was my turn to walk the point. But on that particular morning I had a bad headache and therefore requested that someone else take the point instead. My squad leader gave the position to a guy who had only been in Vietnam for a couple of days. He was hardly the person I would have chosen to lead us, but they didn't ask for my opinion, so I said nothing. I was just glad someone else was doing it and I didn't have to. It took a lot of concentration to walk point and I couldn't do a good job of it with my head pounding from a headache. Therefore, on that day I was the fifth man back from the point.

    As the new rookie started off, I noticed that he was walking too fast and carrying his M-16 by its handle, like it was a briefcase. That was hardly the way for a pointman to act, but he was too far in front of me to say anything. I usually walked slowly and carried my rifle in the ready position on fully automatic, knowing that my only hope for survival as the pointman would be determined by my ability to get the first shot off before my enemy did.

    We had only gone about 100 yards from our base camp when the new rookie at point went around a large twelve-foot high boulder. "CRACK, CRACK, CRACK." It was the awful sound of an AK-47. We all hit the ground as we saw the rookie Marine fly backwards into the bushes in front of us. He had been hit. The corpsman rushed to his side while the rest of us set up a hasty defense. We looked in vain for the sniper. As the corpsman worked on the rookie's chest wounds we all sat quietly in the dense jungle, listening. He was hit by two of the three bullets. One round penetrated his lung and the other one caught a corner of his heart. Every time we tried to move him his heart would stop and the corpsman would have to do CPR. It took us about an hour to get him back to the base camp where a chopper could get to him. During this whole process all I could think about was how glad I was that it was him and not me. I was so thankful for my headache that day. I knew I shouldn't feel that way and I felt guilty, as if somehow the rookie's death was entirely my fault. I listened as he struggled for life. He died just as we got him to the helicopter. He was only eighteen years old.

Those haunting questions returned in full force that day and I couldn't shake them off.

Why am I here?
Is this all there is to life?
What is the purpose of life?
Is there a God?
What happens when we die?

Those questions seemed to demand an answer, but I didn't have any answers. Yet just having the questions rolling around in my mind without the appropriate answers was enough to cause me to begin a search that would eventually change my whole life.

11

C. A. P.

One day we received word that we were to have some visitors on our mountaintop: a chaplain and a barber. Most of us were not too excited about either one. The last thing most of us cared about was our hair, which hadn't been washed in two weeks. However, those in command wanted their troops to look good for the NVA and any friendly generals that might pop in at any moment. The chaplain's visit was supposed to be a boost to our morale. I couldn't understand how a religious nerd would help to boost anyone's morale, but once again, no one consulted me for my advice.

When they arrived, we were informed that everyone would see the barber. The chaplain was optional. I went to both. The chaplain had a worship service in the field and I was surprised at the number of guys that showed up. I don't remember what he preached on except that it seemed inappropriate for us, all things considered. Here we were fighting for our very lives and this chaplain was talking about love and caring for others. We were hoping that maybe he could help us make some sense out of all this, or at least give us something to hope for. I walked away confused. The best thing the chaplain did was to give out pocket size New Testaments. I took one, but I couldn't understand it's Shakespearean language. I was turned off by the "hithers" and "thithers" which didn't seem relevant to my generation. No one in my company seemed to know much about God or Jesus. If we weren't talking about how to stay alive we were talking about home, not about God. God seemed far away, if He existed at all. My New Testament became more of a good luck charm than a book with answers to life's problems. Some guys told stories of how these small Bibles helped to stop bullets and shrapnel. It was encouraging to know that they were good for something.

One day my Sergeant came over to our position and asked if anyone wanted to volunteer for a new job with the Combined Action Program. He told us straight out that it was a suicide mission because the C. A. P. teams often got overrun by the enemy. I volunteered. He took my name, but I really never thought anything would come of it.

After being in the mountains for 31 days we were allowed a short visit back to our Da Nang base camp for resupply. We were escorted by tanks and other armored vehicles. We must have been quite a sight. We hadn't taken a shower for over a month, all the polish on our boots was worn off, our clothes were faded and smelly, and we walked on that base like we were taking over. No one got in our way. As I walked toward my hooch, I noticed some spit-shine new rookie types watching us. I thought back to the day I arrived in Vietnam. Now I looked like a hardened combat vet. My wish had come true.

I never thought a shower would feel so good. I had to really scrub my skin to get the filth off. I had developed some "jungle rot" on my legs and feet. It would take more than a little soap to get that off, yet it felt great just to be out of the bush. The next stop was the mess hall for some hot chow and cold milk. During this past operation we had to go without food for three days because the enemy had us pinned down and the resupply choppers couldn't get near us. Being in the bush helped us to appreciate the things in life we usually took for granted: running water, toilets (even outhouses), showers, hot food, entertainment and our bunks with the flimsy mattresses.

The next morning we were informed that we would be going back out in the bush within 48 hours. This time we would be flown in by choppers. Everyone was slightly bummed out that we had to go back out so soon. What a way to begin the day! Those 48 hours went by fast. Soon we were on the choppers heading out for some unknown region where "Charley" was supposed to be.

We landed without contact with the enemy and moved to a point about four clicks from the LZ (landing zone) for the night. Several days later,

C. A. P.

I got word that I would be flying out the next morning for a two week C. A. P. School. I was excited. I was tired of the infantry and saw C.A.P. as a ray of light. I was afraid that something would happen to hinder me from going, but my final night with the 7th Marines was quiet. When morning came I climbed aboard a Freedom Bird. As they changed the pitch of the rotor blades and we ascended up towards the clouds, I watched the base camp become smaller and I wondered if I would ever see any of those guys again. I was flown to the old base to gather my gear and sign out of the unit. Then I was taken to Da Nang.

The C.A.P. School was located right on the beach, not far from the in-country R & R base called China Beach. The school was built on a small compound not much larger than a football field, but to me it looked like heaven. There were about thirty of us who would be attending the school. We were to receive training not only in C.A.P. unit operations but also in Vietnamese culture. It was totally different from the main mission of search and destroy that I had just left in the infantry unit. C.A.P. sounded like the kind of job we were sent to Vietnam to do: help the Vietnamese people.

Historically, Vietnam had been occupied for close to a thousand years by people from many neighboring countries. The Vietnamese, therefore, had elements of many different cultures that had become a part of their own. There were a lot of different religions in Vietnam including Christianity, Confucianism, Shintoism and Buddhism. Vietnam was a relatively poor, backward country when compared to most modern western nations. The majority of the people were farmers who just wanted to be left alone to grow their rice and raise their families.

Our mission in C.A.P. was to assist the local people to protect themselves from the NVA and Viet Cong who would come into their villages and steal their food, rape their women and brutalize the people by forcing the young men to join with them in their fight against the Americans. If the young men refused, their families would be tortured and killed in front of them. Therefore, they usually gave in and became part of the rebel force.

From the Point to the Cross

C.A.P. began in 1965 around Phu Bai as a part of the initial program of sending advisors into Vietnam. The plan involved taking about five to eight Marines and one Navy corpsman into a village to live with the people. All the villages had a local group of young men (similar to our National Guard) that we were to train in the specifics of war, using our weapons, and techniques. We taught them how to run patrols and set up ambushes, and then we went out with them night after night for the practical application aspect of their training. The C.A.P. program was started as a joint effort between the Green Berets and some special South Vietnamese Soldiers. The idea was to use the Marines to help duplicate what the Green Berets had already been doing, living in the villages with the people and acting as advisors.

I was impressed with the program when I was at the school, but when I finally reached the village (between Phu Bai and Hue) it lost some of its luster. I discovered that the young men we were to train were not totally trustworthy. We always wondered if they were the enemy or friendlies. The village people had lived under warlike conditions so long that they were tired of it. Most of them were nice to us but it was evident that they didn't want us there. I tried to be kind and friendly to everyone, but I always watched my back. I found out later that of the 5,500 Marines who served in C.A.P units while in Vietnam, only half would live to tell about it. The half that did live would return home and face rejection, ridicule and harassment.

After being in my C.A.P. unit for just a little over a month, we received word from headquarters that they were looking for volunteers to attend

Vietnamese language school in Da Nang. The school was a one-month crash course on the basics of the language that involved learning over a thousand commonly used words. Anyone could apply, but they had to have a high IQ with an aptitude for languages. I applied and somehow came down on orders to attend. The school was held at the C.A.P. compound where I took my initial class work. The classes were taught by Vietnamese soldiers and ran all day long and often into the night. I had a great time and learned enough Vietnamese to carry on short conversations. After learning the basics, we

C. A. P.

were expected to return to our villages and pick up more of the language on our own. I returned with high hopes of doing just that. However, when I returned to my village, I was introduced to our new interpreter, a boy about ten who was fluent in French, Vietnamese, and English.

During the daytime our C.A.P. unit (3-1-7) usually took it easy by playing cards or sleeping. However, the masses of flies made it difficult to do either. At night we sent out small patrols of four or five men who would set up an ambush somewhere at the village limits. The rest of the team would find a place to bed down for the night and wait for word from the men that were out on patrol. It was scary walking through the village at night. The dark trails played tricks on our eyes. Most nights were quiet and without incident, but some nights we could just sense danger in the air. We had learned to pay close attention to our environment and all of our senses, including gut feelings.

I was allowed to serve in three different C.A.P. units, all of which were located around Phu Bai, just off Highway One (the only main highway connecting the whole country and built by the Americans). There were moments when it was very rewarding and other times when it was frustrating. One of the good points of the program was getting to know the people. Many of those we came to help saw us every day. We often ate in their homes and played with their children. Every other month or so we would offer a free medical clinic in the village. Our medics, along with any doctors, nurses, or dentists we could find came to the village and cared for the medical needs of the people. It was a great opportunity to show love and compassion. We

wanted them to know we were there to help, and not to hurt them or steal what belonged to them, like so many other soldiers had done.

But there were also many scary moments. Just walking through the village at night was scary enough, but knowing there could be booby traps or ambushes waiting for us put all of us on edge. Yet if we were observant, we could often tell when there was trouble brewing. I remember one night we made our way to the designated location for the evening, but it was obvious that something was wrong. They knew we were coming and someone was waiting for us, I could just feel it. All the houses were empty and no one was around. The animals were even gone. We were walking into a trap. I wanted to turn back, but I wasn't in charge so we continued. With each step I was looking for enemy movement and wondering in the back of mind who set us up. Our plans were usually revealed ahead of time to all of the Americans on the team, as well as to the leaders of the Vietnamese soldiers that we worked with. For all we knew the whole village could end up knowing our every move once our Vietnamese counterparts were told. That certainly seemed to be the case on this night.

We arrived at our destination safely and without incident. But we were on full alert that night. At about 10:30 that night we got hit. I don't even remember how it all started. Bullets just suddenly started pouring into our location. We spread out and started firing back. I grabbed a L.A.W. and fired at a schoolhouse where the enemy seemed to be firing from. Then I got on the radio and called in to our headquarters asking for artillery support. I discovered in that moment just how difficult it is to talk calmly on a radio when people are shooting directly at you. After about ten minutes of intense fighting, it was all over. We had blown up a schoolhouse with a combination of L.A.W.'s and artillery rounds and we had fired hundreds of rounds of ammunition. This time we had no casualties on our side. However, our Vietnamese counterparts had disappeared. I couldn't help but wonder, if these Vietnamese soldiers will run and hide during a fire fight when we are right there with them, what will happen when we leave the country and they have to fight alone? I knew the answer.

Our schedule was pretty consistent – during the day we would lay low and prepare for the evening. At night we would always send out a team of 4 to 6 people on patrol. Those of us who stayed back were the reinforcements in case they came under enemy fire. This sort of thing went on every day, week after week, month after month. The only change was during the monsoon season when we would have to walk around in waist deep water due to the heavy rains. The C.A.P. unit allowed most so us to do what we came to Vietnam to do – help the Vietnamese people.

However, as time went on, I began to resent the very people I was supposed to protect. Many of them seemed to be ungrateful and often acted as if they couldn't care less if we were there or not. My discouragement led me to start counting the days and even the hours before my tour in Vietnam would end. But the closer I got to that date, the more jittery I became. Stories were told of guys who got killed the night before they were supposed to go home. Therefore, during my final 30 days, I never put down my rifle and would usually have at least two or three grenades with me wherever I went. Knowing that most of the action usually took place at night, I didn't want to go to sleep at night. But my eyes would get so heavy that I couldn't keep them open. Yet my nervous tension even caused me to walk in my sleep a few times.

One morning my sergeant came over to where I was sleeping and said, "Hey, Slattery, do you want to go home or not? Get out of bed. I just got word that you are to report to our headquarters in Phu Bai for processing to go home. So what are you waiting for?"

That was all the advance warning I needed. I threw everything together and cautiously made my way through the village for the last time. My rifle was loaded and ready in case anyone tried to get me before I left. I walked quickly to Highway 1 where I caught a ride to Phu Bai. I reported in and had to begin the process of checking out. It took me several days. My next stop was Da Nang where I had to await my plane for Okinawa.

When I arrived in Okinawa I met some guys from my old infantry unit. They told me that only about 25 of the 200 men we had come to Vietnam with had made it. My old battalion had been overrun just a couple of days after I left and about half the men were killed and many more were wounded. Out of the 25 that had made it, over half of us had been wounded at least once. For some reason, none of us felt that the reason our friends had given their lives was worth the price it had cost them.

We put on our dress uniforms with all the new medals we received from our combat experiences and slowly climbed on the buses that drove us out to a Freedom Bird headed for America.

12

GOING HOME

"Gentlemen, the captain has turned on the 'No Smoking' sign as we make our final approach to San Francisco. We would ask that you place your tray tables in their upright positions and please make sure that your seat belts are securely fastened."

When the wheels touched down at Travis Air Force Base everyone cheered. We were HOME. Some of the soldiers kissed the ground when they got off the plane to symbolize, in some small way, how they felt about America. Even with all of its bad points, America was still a great country, and we were all exuberant about being back in this land we called home.
As we made our way to the terminal, most of us were thinking about finding the nearest phone, but first we had to find our gear and go through customs. Surprisingly, the military moved us through very quickly and then let us go.
I joined three other guys to split the cab fare to the nearest airport. Everything seemed new and exciting: the sights, the sounds, and even the traffic. It was a beautiful day. The sun was shining and there was a gentle breeze coming in from the ocean. What a great day to be alive! No one was shooting at us. We were safe. We were back in America.
Yet as I relaxed in the taxicab, it dawned on me that everything was too much the same. Life had gone on without us. The people acted like

there wasn't even a war going on in Vietnam. No one seemed to care. The more I thought about that the more upset I became. Those of us returning from Vietnam didn't receive any type of welcome home celebration. There were no marching bands, no parades, and no special greeting of any kind. We were just a bunch of military men returning from some far away land, fighting a war that no one cared about. We felt like it was our war not theirs. It was weird.

We arrived at the airport, unloaded our baggage and headed for the ticket counter. When I had my ticket in hand I called home.

"Dad? This is Denny. I'm home."

I made arrangements to be picked up at the Detroit airport and then headed for the terminal gate. I had less than an hour before departure. It felt great to be back in America, yet strange at the same time. Vietnam now seemed like a country on another planet because it was so different from life in America.

I was in a daze during the whole flight to Detroit. When the plane touched down my dad was there to meet me along with his new wife, Jan, whom I had never met. The first thing we did was to sit down and have a drink in celebration. I was very tired, but they had a lot of questions about Vietnam and the war. Eventually, I convinced them that I was eager to get home and out of my uniform, so we gathered my bags and headed for my hometown of Jackson, Michigan.

As we drove down those familiar roads I was in awe. Never had I appreciated the beauty of Michigan as I did that day. Before my trip to Vietnam, I would speed down those roads without even paying any attention to the splendor all around me. I was young and in a hurry. But when I was in Vietnam, I would often dream about seeing these familiar sights again. How great life seemed at that moment.

I spent that night with my dad and his new family in a house I had never been in. The next day I went to see my mom and my younger sister, Vicki. When I walked in the house we hugged each other and cried. They treated me like I was a hero, though I didn't feel like a hero. I was just a guy who did his job in a war zone and made it back home alive to tell about it.

We spent several hours talking and then I made a phone call to my old girlfriend. She said she'd like to see me, so I drove over to her house. Things were kind of awkward between us after not seeing each other for over a year. She acted really different. Just listening to her talk made me realize that she had become quite a woman of the world. She was no longer a young naive high school student.

I left her house bewildered. She used to be such a sweet girl. One year had made a big difference in her life. Yet as I drove away from her house, it dawned on me that I too had changed quite a bit during the past year. I was no longer the same naive young punk that she had known. The war had aged me. I had a whole different outlook on life. I was twenty years old, but I felt like I was 50. I viewed all of life differently.

During my 30-day leave I visited some of my friends who had chosen to go on to college in order to avoid the draft. Most of them had long hair and were potheads or tripping on LSD. I didn't fit in with them. I was not interested in the same things. I felt a need to start a new life with new friends who didn't know the old Denny.

When I was in Vietnam I had three goals that I wanted to accomplish if I made it back in one piece:

1. Buy a Corvette
2. Date a lot of beautiful women
3. Go to college

With my dad's help I bought a slightly used 1968 blue Corvette. I felt that having a Corvette would greatly enhance my ability to meet a lot of beautiful women. I'm not sure if it was my charm, the Corvette, or just dumb luck, but I did meet a lot of beautiful women. Therefore two of my goals were accomplished while I was still on leave. The other goal had to be put off until my release from the Marines.

However, in spite of being safely back home, I was having trouble sleeping. I would often jump out of bed at the slightest sound in the house, searching desperately for my weapon, just as I had done so many times in Vietnam. I moved so quickly from a sleeping position to a fighting standing position that I startled anyone who came near me. Then there were the reoccurring nightmares which hindered me from feeling safe and rested. It was like my body was back home, but my mind was still in Vietnam.

I also struggled with anger. I was angry with the Vietnamese for killing so many of my friends, angry with my own government for sending us to Vietnam, angry at the military for putting us in harms way, and angry with the American people for not honoring those of us who made it back alive. I felt like a freak in a sideshow. People who knew me would ultimately ask me how many people I had killed in Vietnam. It seemed like that was all they were interested in. What was I supposed to say? "Oh, man, I slaughtered them by the thousands." In truth, I didn't have any idea. I knew I fired a lot of bullets at the enemy and I threw a lot of grenades and fired some rockets and called in artillery on enemy sites many times but I really didn't keep score. I did what I had to do to survive. I liked the attention, but I resented their questions. I felt like no one really cared or even understood how I felt. Many of my friends had demonstrated in peace rallies as their way of expressing themselves regarding the war in Vietnam. But by telling me of their protest I felt like they were really demonstrating against me. It seemed like they were blaming me for the whole war.

By the time my thirty days of leave were over, I was ready to return to the Marines. Perhaps with other Marines who had been to Vietnam I could feel some form of camaraderie. I signed in at Camp Lejune, North Carolina and unpacked my things. Over the next few days, I met other Marines who shared similar horror stories of their receptions at home. Wives were living with other men, girlfriends had found new boy friends, jobs were filled by other people, and relatives just didn't know how to treat Vietnam Vets. We felt like we were no longer welcomed even in our own homes or the towns we had been raised in. The only place most of us felt understood was in the military. The strange twist to that was that many of us were ticked off at the military too. Yet it was to the military that we ran and it was there that we eventually found refuge.

But I soon discovered that stateside duty was no place for a combat veteran. I wasn't into spit-shine inspections and being hassled. It seemed so irrelevant after a year in combat. So when an opportunity to go on a Mediterranean Cruise came along, I signed up.

Next stop: Europe.

13

GETTING OUT

We arrived at Norfolk, Virginia late in the afternoon. I had never been on a large ship and felt a little apprehensive about being out in the middle of the ocean. That was one of the reasons why I didn't join the Navy—all that water and what lived in that water.

I was assigned to the USS Chilton, which would be the flagship for the fleet. There were five ships in our fleet with about 1,000 Marines scattered between the ships. The hallways were very narrow and there were hatchways all over the ship that we frequently bumped our heads on or stumbled over. All the Marines were put into huge open bays in the bottom of the ships. Our bunks were stacked about ten high with only eighteen inches separating each bunk. I was fortunate enough to grab the top bunk.

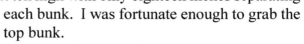

It wasn't long before our ship got underway and we all went to the upper deck to watch the shoreline get further and further away. It was at that point that each man was told to grab a life jacket because we were heading into a storm. The storm turned out to be minor in comparison with what I had envisioned, although by morning probably fifty percent of the Marines were sick. I was one of the fortunate few that did not get sick and was I ever glad I was sleeping on the top bunk that night.

It took us about eight days to get across the Atlantic Ocean. There wasn't much to see except a lot of water and a few dolphins or sharks. My favorite time of day was after the evening meal. I would grab a cup of hot coffee and go to the bow of the ship. I enjoyed feeling the gentle breeze blowing in my face and listening to the sound of the water below being pushed aside by the contours of our ship. The sunsets were beautiful.

During the daytime the Marines were formed into work details, which usually consisted of chipping paint and then applying new paint to the same spot. It seemed like we painted the whole ship several times during our five-month cruise. At night we would usually be free to watch a movie or do whatever we wanted. The food was excellent and they always allowed us to have seconds.

Our first stop was Rota, Spain. We were excited to get off the ship and visit some of the local sights, restaurants and bars. Our greeting party at the dock usually consisted of pimps, prostitutes and local merchants who claimed they could get us anything we wanted from switchblades to tanks. Most of us tried to get away from the dock to see some of the country.

We went on from Spain to visit France, Italy, Greece, several islands in the Mediterranean and then back to Spain. Our mission in the area was to be an evacuation force for American citizens who were visiting or working in the Middle East. We also did some training with the French, Italian and Greek military forces.

When our ship pulled into Rota, Spain for our final stop I began to have severe pains on my left side and back. The pains were such that I couldn't even stand up. I was taken to the dispensary where they discovered I had kidney stones. I was flown to Wiesbaden Air Force Hospital in Germany where I spent the next month waiting for the stone to pass through my urinary track. Most of the time I was fine and able to do anything. It was only when the stone started moving that I would double up in pain. The doctor recommended that I drink plenty of water, coffee and beer to help pass the kidney stones. He also recommended that I change my diet so that I avoid calcium, which also meant that I should stay away from milk, cheese, and dairy products. Many years' later doctors would discover that people with Kidney Stone problems need more calcium in their diet and not less. But at the time I followed the doctor's advice, especially about the beer. If

Getting Out

it would help me avoid that pain then it was worth it. Besides, I was under doctor's orders to drink plenty of beer. I was lucky I didn't turn into an alcoholic.

When the month was up, I was flown to the Great Lakes Naval Hospital, just north of Chicago. I passed the stone in some airport on the way home. Five weeks later, I was given an honorable discharge from the Marines as part of an early out program for Vietnam vets with less than a year left on their enlistment.

I was glad to be out of the Marines and felt ready for civilian life. I knew one of the first things I needed to do was to get a job. I put in an application at Clark Equipment in Jackson, Michigan, and much to my delight, I was hired on the spot as a lathe operator. I then found an apartment and tried to settle down to normal living. I felt like I had everything I needed: a good job, a Corvette, a nice apartment and a lot of female companionship. But inside I felt like something was missing and I didn't know what it was.

I wanted to enjoy life and I didn't want to be tied down. Because of that attitude I went from one girl to another, thinking only of satisfying myself. I felt like America owed it to me as payback for serving in Vietnam. I had always enjoyed dancing and found that it was a great way to meet girls, so I frequented the places that provided dancing and females. I didn't care about anyone. In spite of this attitude, I lived under the delusion that there was one perfect girl who could satisfy my every need. Yet at the same time, I wouldn't let anyone get close enough to me emotionally to find out if they were that special someone. I was confused and hurt deep within. I didn't really know what I wanted out of life.

It was during this time that Connie, one of the girls I dated, came back to me saying she was pregnant. Our relationship had only lasted a couple of weeks, but I knew it was possible that I could be the father of her child. Marriage seemed out of the question for us at the time, but that didn't stop little Kescia from being born on July 24, 1971.

That was a confusing time in my life. I had no seniority at my job and had been laid off twice in six months, so I decided to go back into the military. Believing that variety is the spice of life, I decided to try the Air Force this time. They seemed a little more civilized and from what I had seen, they usually had the best of everything. But when I applied they took one look at my DD-214 discharge papers and said they couldn't use me because my reenlistment code was not a "1A." However, I went to the Army recruiter and they were happy to reenlist me right away. Later, I discovered that my reenlistment code, which kept me out of the Air Force, indicated that I was released from the Marines because I was PREGNANT! I'm sure the clerk who typed my discharge papers got a big laugh out that one. However, when I discovered it, I didn't laugh. Instead it was a legal roadblock that kept me from being in the Air Force. Yet from the Army's perspective, they didn't seem to care if I had been pregnant while in the Marines or not. They never even asked me how I defied nature by getting pregnant in the first place. Instead they just swore me in and sent me to Ft. Gordon, Georgia to be retrained in electronics and work for NSA. However when I arrived the class I was supposed to attend was canceled and I was reassigned to be an electronics expert for navigational systems on helicopters.

It was while I was attending that school at Ft. Gordon that I met Sally. Sally was a beautiful young lady with long blonde hair, who attended the local community college and had a love for flying. We spent a lot of time together and even spoke of getting married someday. One night Sally and I decided to go to a movie called *For Pete's Sake*. The newspaper ad said that it was a different kind of love story. As the film began, Billy Graham came on and I almost walked out. I wasn't interested in religion. I swore under my breath, but Sally convinced me to stay. The story was about a man named Pete who was searching for meaning and purpose in life after his wife had died. I was able to identify with his struggle to such an extent that by the time the film was over, I was quite moved. Just then a man came out on the stage and asked people who felt they needed what Pete (the character in the movie) had found, to respond by coming forward and asking Christ to forgive them. Sally and I sat there talking about our feelings. We both wanted to accept Jesus Christ but we held back. We walked away saying we needed more time to think about it.

Later that same week we saw a new TV show called *The Sixth Sense*. It was all about ESP and the occult. Sally and I both really enjoyed it and wondered if that stuff really worked. We decided to do some research of our own. For the next two months we spent all of our available time researching ESP. We even devised our own experiments, trying to read each other's minds. At first we saw very few positive results, but as time went by we appeared to be making some definite progress. Our progress spurred us on to further study and more experiments. We studied ESP, the occult, astrology, hypnosis and even began dabbling in witchcraft and black magic. There were times when our experiments were spooky, yet we continued because we were hungry for the power that the occult seemed to offer. However, as I drove home from Sally's house at night I would often get an eerie feeling like someone was with me in the car. The hair on the back of my neck would stand up on end and fear would grip my heart, but still I went further into the occult.

My electronics training was almost over when my new orders were given to me. I looked at them in shock.

"REPUBLIC OF SOUTH VIETNAM"

"NOoooooooooooooooooooooooooo!"

14

BACK TO NAM

    I was allowed thirty days leave before I had to report to the West Coast for transportation to Vietnam. During my leave I influenced my mom, my younger sister and some of my friends to experiment with witchcraft and the occult. I hated the thought of another tour of duty in Vietnam, so I tried to use the occult to change my orders, but nothing happened. Having to leave my family for another year was very difficult, especially since I was still having nightmares almost every night from my first tour of duty in Vietnam. But orders are orders. Therefore, when my thirty days of leave were up, I reluctantly boarded a plane for California and said good-bye to those I loved not knowing if I'd ever see them again.

    When I arrived in Vietnam in February of 1972, I tried to convince myself that this tour would not be as bad as my first experience. After all, I was not in the infantry anymore. I would be in a rear area taking care of helicopters that flew out to the battle zone and then returned to the safety of our base in the rear when the mission was completed. There in that safe environment I would take care of their electronic problems. It sounded so logical but I wasn't totally convinced.

    I was assigned to Marble Mountain in DaNang, the largest city in the northernmost region of South Vietnam, known to the military as I Corps. There was a large assault helicopter unit there designated as "F Troop—8th Air Cavalry" which became my family for the next twelve months. The first night I was there we received several incoming rockets at about 3:00 A.M. I found that we could expect to be hit almost every week at least two or three of the seven nights.

During that second tour of duty I discovered that there was a totally different war going on in the rear area. It was a battle against boredom, anxiety, depression, and being a sitting duck. The war was currently escalating as more and more American troops were being sent home. Politically we were hoping that we could slowly withdraw from the war and leave the South Vietnamese Army to fight their own battles. Yet what we discovered was that the South Vietnamese Army often retreated as the enemy advanced. Thus, the enemy was winning back much of the territory that American soldiers had fought for with their own blood, sweat, and tears. To the few thousand of us still left in Vietnam, it was something we hated to see. We felt like we were being abandoned by our own fellow Americans. Now our own lives were in jeopardy because there were so few of us left to stand and fight.

My own battle with fear was just as great as it had ever been. I was afraid to die and even more afraid to be maimed for life. I could fight enemy soldiers charging my position, but I couldn't fight rockets and mortars. All I could do was wait until they came and try to hide. It was all part of the psychological aspect of the war. We all dealt with that stress in different ways. Some guys tried to pretend there wasn't a war going on by getting drunk every night at the club, while others turned to drugs. During my first tour of duty in Vietnam, we didn't have much of a problem with drugs. But during my second tour, drugs were everywhere. Roughly 20% of my company was using heroin in some form. The stuff was so powerful it could be smoked like a cigarette. This usually led to "skin poppin'" and then to "mainlining" it in their veins. Our company would hold periodic urinalysis tests in an attempt to find out who was using heroin. Those who were discovered were shipped out to a detox center and given a dishonorable discharge. I think some of the guys took the stuff just to get out of Vietnam, but I tried to keep as far away from it as I could.

I used education, books, movies, supportive friends, and booze to break away from the reality of the war. I hated Vietnam just as much this time as I had the first time. The heat, the rats, the huge flying cockroaches, the uncertainty of the future and the anxiety of the war were more than enough to make all of us want to leave on the next "Freedom Bird" headed for America. I wanted peace and yet I found myself surrounded on every side by a war that we were not allowed to win. I hated it. We were in a "no win "situation. Only later would we learn that Buddhist Monks, occult practners, and other Vietnamese religious leaders were daily praying to their gods and demons that American soldiers would not only lose the war but be defeated in life. They put curses and hexes on us every day we were in their country. They continually asked spiritual forces to make sure that we would be restless wanderers searching for an illusive peace that would always be just out of our reach.

For me the days turned into weeks and the weeks gradually turned into months. I wrote to Sally almost every day but as time went on I began to notice that her letters were no longer showing up every day and the content became more distant instead of intimate. Then one day a letter arrived saying that she thought it was best for us to split up. That was the second "Dear John" letter I received, one for each tour. I wasn't as surprised the second time. Most of the men almost expected their wives and girl friends to be unfaithful while they were gone, but at the same time they prayed it wouldn't happen.

In October of 1972, we were moved south to Bien Hoa. It was there that three men began to have an impact on my life. They all claimed to be Christians, although one lived a more vile life than I did. His big thing was to sleep with two prostitutes at a time. One of the other Christians walked a straight path and lived a very disciplined life. Tim Hall was the third guy and he seemed to be kind of in the middle.

In the past, I had not been very open to talking about spiritual things. I had concluded that the church was full of hypocrites, like the guy in my unit who was into prostitutes. Having been raised in the church, I felt I had explored all that the church had to offer and rejected it as irrelevant, powerless, and boring. However, my experience with the occult had caused me to rethink things. I knew there was an evil power that was beyond my reasoning, so I assumed there must also be good forces in some invisible realm.

One guy in my unit spoke of a deeper experience I could have that would fill the void in my life. He spoke of having meaning and purpose in life through Jesus. Then he told me that the Bible contained the answers to life's most probing questions. That comment struck a chord in my heart

because I was looking for answers to some tough questions that had been bothering me since my first tour in Vietnam:
Why am I here?
Is this all there is to life?
What is the purpose of life?
What happens when we die?
Is there a God?

This radical Christian challenged me to read the Bible. I had rejected the Bible when I was just ten years old because it seemed to be out of touch with real life. I got lost in all the "Hithers" and "Thithers." It didn't make any sense in our modern world and I was very quick to let my friend know just how I felt.

"Hey, dude, the Bible is irrelevant today. It was written over 2,000 years ago by a bunch of old guys. This is the 20th century and times have changed. The Bible is filled with old fashioned ideas that don't make sense in the world today."

My friend said, "I'm telling you that this Book has the answers to the questions that you are asking."

"Oh, really? Then show me anything that is relevant in that old book."

"OK. Just open it anywhere."

He handed me a Bible and I just let it fall open to the middle book of Proverbs. I looked down the page and stopped about half way down to the first verse that caught my eye. I was expecting to find a "Hither" or "Thither" so I could throw the book at him, but instead I just stood there dumbfounded with my mouth open. I was shocked as I looked at the verse in front of me. I read it over and over and was stunned by its simplicity. I realized then that I had come face to face with truth, for there before me was a verse that actually made sense. All my arguments about God being out of touch with the real world were decimated. I had reasoned in my own mind that if God existed then surely He would have some understanding of what life was like for us in this crazy modern world. Now before me was the proof. I had discovered the most powerful verse in the Bible but it wasn't until much later that I would find out it is so important that it is in the Bible three times.

"It is better to live in the corner of an attic than in a beautiful home with a cranky and quarrelsome woman."
(Proverbs 25:24 - Living Bible)

As I read that verse the only thing I could say was, "Amen! Now that's truth!" I knew enough about life to know that if I spent time around a cranky and quarrelsome woman, she would ruin my whole day or my whole life if I married her. I was shocked that something from the Bible actually made sense. As I stood there with that Bible in my hands I began to wonder if there were other verses in the Bible that might also make sense. As I began to flip the pages for more nuggets of truth, I was amazed to find them everywhere. How could I have been so blind not to have seen it before? I had never even given the Bible a chance. Could it be that God really did have the answers to my questions?

Tim Hall gave me his Bible so I could read it in my spare time. My Christian friends talked to me about the Lord every day. When we went to the mess hall to eat we actually prayed over our food. Soon there were other men who were interested in joining us and so our small group expanded.

As I studied the Bible I discovered that Jesus promised He would return to this earth some day in the future. No one knew exactly when, but the Bible gave us some signs to look for, such as; wars, famine, earthquakes, unrest among the nations, the rise of a world dictator, and eventually nuclear explosions. Jesus was coming for two reasons:

1. To judge the Devil, the Anti-Christ and all inhabitatants of the earth
2. To gather together His followers and take them to heaven

No one had to tell me that I was not a follower of Jesus Christ. I had often cursed Him and His followers. But now I was beginning to see that I was on the wrong team. My involvement in the occult had convinced me that the devil was real. I knew that if there was a real devil, there had to be a real God. It all seemed so clear. Why didn't I ever see it before? It was almost as if I had been blinded to the truth, while desperately searching for it.

Well, one thing I did know, fooling around with the occult was wrong. How I arrived at that decision I wasn't sure. But I decided to take all my books, tapes, records, hypnotizing wheels, and all the other occult paraphernalia I had with me and burn it in the trash bin. It was actually fun doing it. The things I thought would give me power and self-fulfillment were going up in flames and I felt good about it. It just seemed like the right thing to do at the time.

As the sun was setting that night and darkness began to surround us, I walked away from the fire and bowed on my knees in an open field and looked up into the dark sky. There I prayed the first real prayer I could ever remember praying,

"God, if you're real, somehow prove it to me. I want to know you. Do something to convince me that you exist. I don't want to play any games, so I ask you to prove to me that you exist and then I'll believe in You."

The night was dark and silent, yet in that moment of time, the war seemed far away. I couldn't tell if anything happened when I prayed. I didn't receive any sign, or hear a voice, or see lightening strike the earth or even hear the rumbling of a distant thunder. The earth didn't shake and my heart didn't stop beating. There was just a calm silence. Yet when I rose to my feet, somehow I knew that God did exist and that He had heard my prayer and that He would answer me in ways far beyond anything I could even imagine.

15

WRESTLING WITH QUESTIONS

    Rumors were spreading that the war was going to end soon. Those of us serving in Vietnam hoped more than anyone else that those rumors were true. This war had already turned out to be the longest war that America had ever been involved in. Those of us doing the fighting hated it because it was a war that we were not allowed to win. We wanted to either invade North Vietnam and get it over with or get out. Too many lives had already been lost for us just to continue doing what we had been doing.

    Toward the end of January we heard that the Paris Peace Talks were actually making progress. A cease fire was set to begin on Sunday January 28, 1973. On Monday the *Stars & Stripes* newspaper carried the headline - - "It's All Over". When the news reached us some of our pilots got in their choppers and flew crazy patterns over the base, firing rockets and flares to simulate fireworks used back home for Fourth of July celebrations. That day we thought President Nixon was the greatest man alive for getting us out of Vietnam.

    The pull-out of Americans began immediately. We left all kinds of equipment and supplies for whoever wanted them. We were told it was being given to the South Vietnamese Army but quite frankly, we didn't care. We just wanted to get out of Vietnam while we could. We feared that the

Vietnamese would retaliate as they watched us get on our trucks to leave. Their future looked very dim as Americans pulled out enmasse.

Within a few days, I was at Tan Son Nhut airport in Saigon, climbing on a Jet headed for America and holding on tightly to my boarding pass. As I looked out the window of that freedom bird I said, "Good-bye Vietnam. Never again!"

It was a happy moment for all of us when we landed in San Francisco. Cheers went up from all over the plane. We were home. America had never looked better. Once we were off the plane we were ushered into a mess hall for a big steak dinner. It was the military way of saying "Welcome Home". The steak was great but most of us just wanted to get home to our families. As soon as possible I got a cab for the airport with a couple of other guys. On the way to the airport a song came on the radio, *"Do you know the way to San Jose, I've been away so long..."* Just as I heard those words I saw a sign for San Jose on the freeway and I thought how appropriate those words were. Yeah, I've been away so long and it's good to be back. This time I knew what to expect.

My mom met me at the airport. Since the next day was Sunday, I asked her if she'd like to go to church with me. I felt I owed something to God for getting me home safely twice. I had made a silent commitment to God to study the Bible, even though I still intended to live like the devil.

While I was in Vietnam I had decided that if I made it back to the States alive I would take responsibility for Kescia, who was now nearly two years old. Therefore, one of the first places I visited while on leave was the Jackson County Building, Friend of the Court office. It seemed like they were a little surprised to see me. I told them who I was and that I wanted to begin paying child support for Kescia. Blood tests were taken and a court date set. In court I agreed to pay the set amount of child support. Before I left for my next duty station I even went by to see Kescia and her mother. Kescia was as cute as a button, but Connie and I weren't on the same wave length, so marriage still seemed out of the question. It was obvious that Connie hated me and in her eyes, I would always be a creep. There was nothing I could do to change the past, yet I felt guilty as I walked away.

I had a lot of questions rolling around in my mind by the time I arrived at my next duty station, Ft. Knox, Kentucky. My job classification (MOS) indicated that I was an electronics technician but the Army often used people wherever they needed them. When I arrived they needed a driver for the

Wrestling with Questions

Battalion Commander, so I became a driver. Driving for a Colonel had some real advantages, such as riding with him in a two man Cobra attack helicopter, better hours, better food, and the fact that no one could touch me for work details.

During off-duty hours I explored the sights of Louisville. I was always on the lookout for girls and one of the best ways of meeting girls I had discovered was through dancing, so I hunted for all the local hangouts. One of the girls that I spent most of my time with, while stationed in the area, was Barb. Barb helped me wrestle with the issues of life. Many of the things I had thought would make me happy didn't. During my stay at Fort Knox, Barb and I went to several movies that addressed my questions like, *Jesus Christ Superstar* and *Godspell*. Another movie I went to see many times was the *Lost Horizon*. It was a wonderful movie about a paradise called Shangri-La. I longed for such a place and the peace it offered, but the lights would always come on at the end of the movie and I would have to go out and face the real world.

Much later, I would discover that there really is a paradise in a place called heaven. The only earthly paradise had been the Garden of Eden until it was stained with sin. The best thing in my life at the time was Barb because she believed in me. But even Barb didn't have the answers to the questions that continued to haunt me:

- What is the purpose of life?
- What happens when we die?
- Why is there suffering in the world?
- How does Jesus fit in?

Somehow I felt the questions were good ones but I didn't know where to even begin looking for the answers. People said the answers were in the Bible, but I didn't know where to look. But with each passing day, I was becoming more desperate for those answers.

My feelings all came to a climax one night as I watched a TV program in the lounge of my barracks. The program dealt with the advances in nuclear technology, giving us the ability to totally demolish the world and every living thing in it with just the touch of a button. They showed graphic illustrations of nuclear bombs exploding.

It reminded me of several Bible passages I had read dealing with the end of the world. There were two passages that really tied into the predictions of a nuclear war :

"But the day of the Lord will come like a thief. The heavens will disappear with a roar; the elements will be destroyed by fire, and the earth and everything in it will be laid bare (burned up)."
(2 Peter 3:10)

"This is the plague with which the Lord will strike all the nations that fought against Jerusalem: Their flesh will rot while they are still standing on their feet, their eyes will rot in their sockets, and their tongues will rot in their mouths."(Zechariah 14:12)

I knew the Bible said to watch for signs of the return of Jesus and as I looked around, it seemed like most of the signs were evident. Furthermore, I knew that if Jesus did return now, I was not ready to meet Him. I was still a sinful man. No one needed to convince me of that, I knew it. I had done so many terrible things in my life that I didn't think I could ever be forgiven by people or God. The Ten Commandments said we shouldn't have any other gods, create idols, misuse God's name, break the Sabbath, dishonor our parents, steal, kill, commit adultery, lie, or covet what others have. I had broken everyone of those commands, as well as many others not on that list. How could God ever forgive me?

The TV program showed many nuclear explosions, while the commentator stated that it could happen anywhere, at any second of any day. I ran outside to my car and wept. I wanted to become a Christian now while there was still time, but I didn't know how. I prayed that night asking for God's help. As I prayed, I thought about a little white church that I passed on the way to my favorite bar. It used to bug me that there were always cars at that church, no matter what night I drove by. I used to think, "Don't those people know church is a drag? What's wrong with them?" Yet that night as I sat in my car weeping, I determined that if I was going to look for answers, maybe I might find them in that little white church.

Having been forced to go to church as a child, I knew what churches were like. However, it was usually a strange feeling walking into a church that I had never been to. I always wondered if they were going to do anything weird. But the next Sunday I walked into that little white church and quickly found a seat. Several people came up and introduced themselves and said how glad they were that I was there. I wasn't impressed with the sermon and I thought it was a little strange that they sang without musical accompaniment. I wasn't sure if I would ever come back, but as I was getting ready to leave after the service, the pastor asked me if I would go to lunch with him the next day and I said "OK."

I showed up for lunch that Monday wondering what the pastor was up to. We made small talk and were just finishing our lunch when he changed gears and started talking about how important it was to be baptized. He pulled out a Bible and showed me several passages that referred to baptism. I tried to explain to him that I had been baptized as a child , but I got the feeling by his reaction that somehow that wasn't good enough. I figured if what I needed in order to get my act together was to be baptized again, then I was all for it. "Let's do it!"

We left the restaurant and returned to his church. He had a huge tub right behind the pulpit that was filled with water. We changed into some different clothes and climbed in the tub. There he baptized me. When we had dried off and changed back into our original clothes, we said our good-byes and I left. The pastor seemed more excited than I was over what had happened. He stood there with a big smile on his face like he had just accomplished a great feat. Truthfully, I wasn't sure what had happened except that I felt cleaner on the outside. I still had no answers to my questions and I felt empty on the inside. I climbed in my car and reflected on what had taken place as I drove to the bar to hustle some girl on the dance floor.

16

<u>GETTING RIGHT</u>

One day I heard that they needed people with avionics training in Korea, so I volunteered to go. When my orders arrived they included some leave time prior to my departure. Barb and I talked about a future together but this time I had cold feet and backed away. We said our good-byes and I headed for Michigan. I love Michigan more than all the other places I have ever been. As I drove into my hometown of Jackson, Michigan, I heard the disc jockey from the local radio station announcing some kind of special concert in Ella Sharp Park. I made a mental note of when it was and decided right then to check it out.

After visiting with my family I made my way over to the park. It looked like about 300 people had gathered for the concert. Most of those in attendance were between 15-35 years of age. The *Good News Circle* sang songs I didn't know but I was impressed with their upbeat joyful sound . Their songs were happy songs that spoke of the love of God and they encouraged the crowd to sing along and clap their hands. Even the audience seemed to beam with a radiance and joy that I lacked. I wanted the peace and confidence they seemed to have.

After singing for about an hour the leader of the group, Bob Laurent, took out a Bible and began to tell a story about three men named Shadrach, Meshach, and Abednego. He told how those men trusted God and were committed to Him so much that they were willing to be thrown into a flaming furnace rather than deny God by bowing down to an idol. The strange part of that story was that God saved them from the flames. The speaker then said that there was a fire awaiting each of us as the penalty for our sin but that God wanted to save us from those flames. In fact, God's love was so great that He sent His only Son, Jesus Christ, to die in our place so that we could be delivered from eternal punishment in Hell. The leader then asked if anyone would like to receive God's way out through trusting in Christ. He invited those who wanted to receive Christ to come to the front for prayer, as the group sang "Just As I Am".

I believed everything he said, yet I sat in that crowd being held back by my own pride. "What will people think of me if I go down there and make a fool out of myself?" As I looked around I saw a lot of attractive young ladies that I would hustle if given the chance. How could I humble myself in front of them? I was literally too "cool" to move.

Inside I wanted to run to the front. Salvation in Christ was everything I had been looking for, yet it was like I was glued to that bench. As others were finding their way to the platform, Bob Laurent came back to the microphone and said, "I feel like we need to sing one more verse of this song. If God is dealing with your heart, give in and come. I just sense someone else is wanting to come but is struggling. Won't you give in to Jesus? He's waiting for you."

A part of me said, "GO" and another part of me said, "Don't be a fool". As I sat there wondering what to do, a woman in front of me turned around, looked right at me and said, "Don't you think you ought to go down there?"

I was stunned. It was as if she knew just what I was thinking. I thought I was in the *Twilight Zone*. I looked at her and then looked toward the stage. I hesitated a few moments and then said, "Oh, what the hell!" With that, I got to my feet and made my way to the front.

When we arrived at the stage we were asked to get on our knees and pray with the leader this prayer:

"Dear God, I come to You as a sinner. I ask You to forgive me for my sins. Jesus, come into my life. I open the door of my heart to You now. Save me, Jesus. I give You my life. Use me for Your glory. Amen."

Getting Right

As I prayed that prayer I didn't feel the earth move nor did I see any visions. Lightning didn't strike and I didn't hear God's voice. But when I got up off my knees I was a different person. I would never again be the same. Jesus had changed my life! I was forgiven for every wrong I had ever done. I felt clean inside. This is what every Vietnam vet needed I thought--forgiveness and a new start. But only God could grant it and to receive it we needed to humble ourselves before the Lord. For many people, men especially, this is a very difficult thing to do. We like to think we can get along on our own because we're tough. We don't need God. That's what I had thought until the night I gave in and asked Christ into my life. I didn't totally understand it at the time, but I would eventually.

When I left the concert, I went straight to my mom's apartment to tell her the good news. She acted happy for me, but I detected a little skepticism. She had seen me go through many fads and she had every right to be skeptical. In her mind, I was just into another fad, the Christian bandwagon. But regardless of her first reaction, over the next few days she watched in amazement as her son read the Bible like it was the most exciting book in the world. I don't think either of us realized the miracle Jesus had performed on a wicked sinner named Dennis Slattery. But in time we would.

17

FOLLOW-UP

After inviting Christ into my life I started to wonder - - "What is a Christian is supposed to do?" "How am I supposed to live?" "What's OK and what's not OK?" To help me deal with those questions I was assigned two counselors from the concert in the park. They were supposed to get with me and help me get off to a good start by teaching me the basics. One of them was a guy about my age named Ray. I called Ray on the phone to ask for help with my questions.

"Hello, Ray? This is Dennis Slattery, from the concert in Ella Sharp Park the other night. Could we get together for some Bible study? I have a few questions I'd like to run by you."

"Well, let me pray about it and I'll get back with you."

I was a little turned off when he said, "Let me pray about it . . ." but I was supposed to learn from him so I figured he knew what he was doing. About 15 minutes later he called and said that it would be OK. We went back to the same park and had our meeting next to a beautiful flower garden. Ray decided the first thing I should learn about was prayer, so for 30 minutes he told me how important it was to pray to God every day. He told me I could talk to God like a regular person and ask Him anything. At the end of the lesson he asked me if I wanted to pray for anything. I said, "Sure," and began to pray;

From the Point to the Cross

"Lord, we are down here trying to study Your Bible and these mosquitoes of yours are tearing us up. Please protect us so we don't get bit any more tonight, in Jesus' name. Amen."

When Ray heard my prayer he tried to lecture me on how wrong it was for me to ask God for those kinds of things. Ray then rambled on talking about something else for another 30 minutes. But as we got up to leave I reminded Ray that we hadn't been bit by any mosquitoes since I had prayed that prayer. He thought of it as a coincidence but for me it was a crucial lesson on the love of God and the power He has to back up His promises. He is never too busy to hear the sincere prayers of His children.

Ray and I met one other time, but we didn't hit it off. I called my other counselor, a girl named Elli. She suggested we play tennis. She hadn't been a Christian very long either and it soon became apparent that she had something more than follow-up on her mind. We only met a few times because I was turned off by her aggressiveness. I wasn't ready for a relationship with any girls at this point in my life. If I was going to learn about the Lord and being a Christian, I would have to learn from someone else.

It was then that I visited a strange place that I usually didn't frequent: Church. I had never really liked Church. To me it was usually very boring and I didn't like sitting still that long, but I thought I'd give it another try. My mom and I went together to a church near her apartment. When I walked in I felt like I was home. I now knew the secret. The Church is for God's family, His kids. Now that I was part of the family, I actually enjoyed it. It made sense to me. After the service I met some of the young people who invited me to a Bible study. I went and had a great time. Afterward the pastor invited me to go to the *Lansing City Rescue Mission* with him to share my testimony. I didn't know what a testimony was, but I went anyway.

The Rescue Mission was in a bad part of Lansing. There were prostitutes outside and bums leaning against buildings. We got out of the car and as we entered the mission we were met by another whole group of bums inside. Just before the meeting got underway I was told that the men and women had to listen to the sermon before they could eat. I looked at the crowd and wondered what I had to offer them. However, when my time came, I got up asking God for wisdom and spoke about what Jesus had done for me. I

Follow-Up

hadn't been that nervous since Vietnam. On the way home the pastor asked me to help him with the junior high kids in Vacation Bible School the next day. I showed up and he turned the class over to me, thus launching my career in ministering to people.

18

BAD HABITS

I had only been a Christian for a few days when I was asked to teach that junior high class. Every night I would stay up until 2:00 or 3:00 A.M. just reading the Bible and trying to figure out what to say to those kids. I didn't know much at that time, but I was very eager to learn.

As I studied the Bible, I became more convinced than ever that I was unworthy of God's grace and love. At times I would just weep uncontrollably as I cried out to God in prayer. I began to view myself as the chief of all sinners, even worse than the Apostle Paul (I Timothy 1:15). I had broken just about every commandment in the Bible so I couldn't understand why God would want anything to do with me. I knew I didn't deserve His love and forgiveness. If I got what I deserved I would burn forever in the flames of Hell. Yet in Christ God forgave me and promised me a place in Heaven. Such love was beyond my comprehension.

Reading the Bible helped me understand Jesus and the sacrifice He had made on the cross. He died in MY place and paid the penalty that I owed to God for my many sins. He did that because it was the only way that I could ever be free. Jesus became not just my Savior and Lord but my friend. I began having in-depth conversations with Him daily. At just the mention of His name, tears would form in my eyes. Jesus became my Hero. I wanted to be like Him, but I was not sure how to do that in the twentieth century. In my estimation, a lot of Christians were weird and seemed to live BORING lives. I couldn't figure out how the children of such a creative God could be such a drag.

I had found THE WAY, THE TRUTH, and THE LIFE. There wasn't anything boring about the Lord or about living for Him. I was excited to be a Christian. In response to His love I wanted to tell everyone I knew what Jesus had done. I talked to my friend, Roger, and his parents about my new relationship with God through Christ. However, I came on a little too strong and they weren't sure at first how to react. When I told my own family, they had the same kind of reaction. My friends and family began to look at me as a kook - - a religious fanatic who had flipped out. As I read the Bible I discovered that Jesus was radical so I wanted to be radical too. I began witnessing to anything that moved and even some things that didn't move. No one told me to, I just wanted to. I would even walk up to trees and say, "Hey tree, God made you!"

On one occasion, I was sharing with a young girl who had been taking mind expanding drugs, like LSD. She began to weep as I told her of Jesus and what He could do for her. In tears she said she wanted Jesus to be her Lord. I told her we had to go to the church I was attending so the pastor could pray with her to receive Christ. When we found the pastor he did lead the girl to Christ but he also told me I could do it myself. He said, "God can hear you pray anywhere."

Only then did it dawn on me that I had received Christ in a park and it had worked for me, so why wouldn't it work for others? From that day on, I was not hindered in leading someone to Christ because we weren't in a church or because there weren't any pastors available. I believed God could hear ME pray ANYWHERE!

Being a radical witness for Christ also seemed to entail getting rid of my bad habits. I had no habitual problem with alcohol or drugs but cigarettes were a BIG PROBLEM! I had been a heavy smoker for nine years. I had tried to quit many times but always without success. After several hours without a cigarette my mouth would just water in anticipation of nicotine. On one occasion, I did quit for about ten days but my mouth, tongue, and lips broke out in so many canker sores that I went to a doctor. His advice to me was that if all the sores in my mouth were caused by the sudden withdrawal of nicotine, then I should start smoking again. As soon as I did all the sores cleared up.

Bad Habits

However, as a recent convert to Christianity, smoking just didn't seem right to me. I tried a few times to quit but without success. I even made vows to God about smoking but ended up breaking all of them. Some Christians made fun of smokers saying, "Smoking may not send anyone to hell but it sure makes them smell like they've been there." Or the sign that reads, "Eternity: Smoking or Non-Smoking?" Since I couldn't kick my habit I did the only respectable thing I could do . . . I decided to hide whenever I smoked. Being in the Army made that even easier because my leave time soon ran out and I had to depart for my next duty station. I said good-bye to my family and new Christian friends and headed for the airport. I walked through the gate leading to my jet for Korea. When our plane eventually got underway and we were lifted into the air, the "No Smoking" sign was turned off and I pulled out a cigarette and lit up.

"Lord, someday please help me quit smoking."

God heard that prayer and even then began to set things in motion to answer it.

19

KOREA

    I arrived safely at Camp Red Cloud in Ui Jong Bu, South Korea. It was located about 20 miles south of the DMZ in a beautiful valley surrounded by mountains. I was assigned to the 128th Aviation. We had a small base about three hundred meters outside the front gate of Camp Red Cloud. I was excited about my new duty station.

    Most of the guys in my unit went to the club every night. Some of them even had live-in girl friends called "YO-BO'S". These were basically prostitutes that were hired to not only provide sexual favors but also to cook, clean, and take care of their man. I tried to spend my free time doing other things but discovered there wasn't much to do during off duty hours.

    The post chapel was dead. I attended the services anyway but only a few people showed up. This was typical of post chapels. I didn't have much respect for the chaplains I'd met. In my opinion they talked about things that nobody cared about. Jesus wasn't like that. He was relevant. Now that I was a Christian I wondered if there were any chaplains who believed in the Lord as I did.

    I didn't know if any of the men in my unit were Christian and I really needed Christian fellowship. Without the encouragement of other Christians I basically started drying up spiritually. I felt like a hot coal that was set aside all by itself. My fire was going out. As the days turned into weeks, I got bored sitting in the barracks every night reading my Bible, so one night

I went with some of the guys to the club. The place was crowded with not only soldiers but also a lot of Korean girls looking for G.I.'s with some money to burn. I started off drinking only pop but ended up having several mixed drinks, just like old times. My one night fling back into the bar scene turned into an every night ordeal. I was sliding back into a sinful life style and didn't know how to stop. I became angry with myself for lacking the discipline to live for the Lord and I got angry with God for letting it happen. I couldn't see how God could forgive me for going back to my old ways, so I didn't seek His forgiveness, but I was miserable. I knew there was a better way to live, but I just didn't know how to do it.

The event that turned my life around came in the form of sickness. It started in the early afternoon as a sore throat and a fever. This was followed by a severe headache and an upset stomach. By 6:00 PM I was almost delirious with hot and cold flashes. It reminded me of a sickness I had struggled with in Vietnam which produced symptoms similar to those associated with malaria. I was writhing in pain and praying for death to come quickly.

"God, I'm no good to anyone like this. If I can't live the Christian life here on earth in a way that pleases You, then just take me home. Either take me home or heal me . . . Jesus, help me."

As I prayed that prayer it seemed like the Lord stepped out of eternity and into my room. I could sense His presence at the bottom of my bunk. I cried out to Him, "Jesus, heal me." As soon as I cried out to Him I began to feel a soothing cloud envelop me. It started at my feet and slowly worked its way up my body bringing relief and healing. When it reached my head, my eyes closed and I fell asleep.

When I woke up the next morning I was fine. I started the day with prayer.

"Lord, I haven't been a very good Christian over here in Korea so far, so I'd like to ask a favor. Could I go back to Michigan for another month to become stronger in my faith? I just feel like I need more time. It's in your hands, in Jesus' name."

That week I received word that my stepfather had died and that I was to go home on emergency leave to attend the funeral. I would be given thirty days leave.

20

POWER FOR LIVING

When I arrived back in Jackson, Michigan I contacted some of my Christian friends and set up a time to get together. They were surprised to see me back so soon since I was supposed to be in Korea for a one year tour. I told them the story and we rejoiced together to see how God had answered prayer.

I never did attend my stepfather's funeral because I arrived one day late. We weren't that close anyway. He had only been married to my mom for about four years and I was gone during most of that time. I saw this trip back as a faith strengthening adventure that God had designed at the Army's expense.

I went to a Bible study on Thursday and met a neat Christian, Lenore. She invited me to another Christian gathering that met on Sunday nights in a gym. As it turned out the gym belonged to St. Mary's Catholic Church. The room where we were to have the meeting was an old gym with basketball hoops on each end. There were chairs set up in a circular format with the leaders and musicians located in the very center. The service started, like most Christian gatherings, with singing, but the songs these people sang were lively and joyous. Some of the people used tambourines to help keep beat with the music, while others clapped their hands. On several occasions, we all hooked arms and swayed while we sang songs of praise to God. God seemed to be very present as we lifted our hearts to Him. At one point in the service the people closed their eyes, lifted their hands toward heaven and sang a strange, beautiful song that I couldn't figure out. It made me feel like I was in heaven listening to angels. When the singing stopped several people had messages that they gave to the group that started with the words, "Thus saith the Lord..." Lenore leaned over and told me that they were using the gift of prophesy. Then the leader stood and gave a sermon on the Spirit-filled life. He finished his message by saying that if anyone wanted to be filled with the Holy Spirit that they should go downstairs to the prayer room. When the final song was sung, I rushed to that room to find out more about this Spirit-filled experience.

The prayer room was simply a classroom that they were using to instruct, counsel, and pray with people. I told them that I wanted to be Spirit-filled, so about ten people gathered around me and laid their hands on me and started to pray. A Catholic priest did most of the praying. He prayed for about five minutes and then stopped because it seemed like nothing was happening. He instructed me to keep seeking to be filled with the Holy Spirit and that God would answer when the time was right. I walked away from that prayer room feeling unworthy to receive from God.

Lenore gave me a book that night to encourage me. It was Pat Boone's life story titled, *A New Song*. I started reading it as soon as I got home. In the book, Pat told how he became a singer and later an actor. However, his career made him compromise his morals and beliefs. Yet God used Pat's acting ability to land the lead part in the movie, *The Cross and the Switchblade*. The movie was based on the true story of a country preacher named David Wilkerson who felt called to the gangs in New York City. David started an organization called "Teen Challenge" that helped drug addicts, prostitutes, pimps, gang members, and other troubled youth get their life together by accepting Christ and learning to live for Him. While they were making the movie Pat Boone was very challenged by David Wilkerson's confidence that Jesus could help anyone. David also spoke frequently about the need to be filled with the Holy Spirit. Their conversations sparked a hunger in Pat Boone for more of God. In one scene, toward the end of the movie, Pat was touched by the Lord in a powerful way. When he finally received the baptism of the Holy Spirit his whole life changed. He started witnessing to people and actually living the Christian life.

By the time I finished reading Pat Boone's book I wanted what he had. I searched the Bible for the verses that he had referred to in his book and became even more convinced that I needed the power of the Holy Spirit in my life. I couldn't figure out why I hadn't heard about this before. I went to the pastor of the church I had been attending and he told me that the Holy Spirit wasn't needed today.

"We don't need miracles and the baptism of the Holy Spirit for today. Those things were only to help establish the early church. Now we have the Bible in its completed form and that's all we need. Stay away from people who tell you otherwise."

I walked away from the pastor's office a little confused. It seemed to me that if the Bible speaks about the baptism of the Holy Spirit as the dynamic power of the church, then why couldn't we have it now? Maybe the pastor didn't need power in his life but I sure needed help in mine. The pastor's advice didn't make sense. I couldn't see why I should stay away from people who seemed to love the Lord. I was confused.

When I got home I opened my Bible to study this subject again.

"If you then, though you are evil, know how to give good gifts to your children, how much more will your Father in heaven give the Holy Spirit to those who ask Him?" (Luke 11:13)

"But you will receive power when the Holy Spirit comes on you; and you will be my witnesses in Jerusalem, and in all Judea and Samaria, and to the ends of the earth." (Acts 1:8)

The book of Acts then records five different times when people received the baptism of the Holy Spirit (Acts 2, 8, 9, 10, 19). All of the books of the New Testament were written BY Spirit-filled Christians and TO Spirit-filled Christians. I Corinthians 12 & 14 deal with the use of the gifts of the Holy Spirit. Why would God include all of those verses in His Bible if it didn't apply to us today? It didn't make sense.

The pastor I talked to had referred to two passages of Scripture as a disclaimer to any modern day version of the baptism in the Holy Spirit. The first verse was found in the book of Romans chapter 8;

"If anyone does not have the Spirit of Christ, he does not belong to Christ."(Romans 8:9)

The pastor said that Christians already have the Holy Spirit according to this verse and I didn't need another experience. However, as I searched the Scriptures I discovered that the early Christians had two experiences. This is most clearly seen in Acts 8: 4-17. Philip preached the gospel in Samaria and the people responded and were baptized in water. Yet Peter and John felt the need to go and share with them about the Holy Spirit several days later. When the apostles laid their hands on the Samaritan Christians they received the Holy Spirit - - a second blessing beyond salvation.

The second passage of Scripture that the pastor referred to was found in the first letter of the Apostle Paul to the Corinthians;

"Love never fails. But where there are prophecies, they will cease; where there are tongues, they will be stilled; where there is knowledge, it will pass away. For we know in part and we prophesy in part, but when perfection comes, the imperfect disappears."
(I Corinthians 13: 8-10)

The pastor told me that this verse meant that when the Bible, in its completed form, was in print then we wouldn't need the baptism in the Holy Spirit and the accompanying gifts. However, it seemed to me that those verses were referring to a future time in heaven when all the things of this earth, except the things of eternal value (faith, hope, and love), will lose their usefulness. For since the Bible is filled with prophecies and knowledge that God feels we need to know to live for Him while on this earth, how could someone say that the Bible with all its prophecies and knowledge is that which is perfect, referred to in this passage? It didn't make sense to me. I couldn't see how someone could say we didn't need the power of the Holy Spirit today.

To me, if anything those verses seemed to say that there will come a time when prophecy, tongues, and knowledge will cease. But it never says what it is referring to as that which is perfect. I thought heaven was the only place where things were perfect. And isn't the Bible filled with knowledge, prophecies, and stories of people who spoke in tongues while under the influence of the Holy Spirit? How could those things now be called evil?

Therefore, I had to conclude that my pastor was wrong. If Jesus said we should ask our Heavenly Father to fill us with the Holy Spirit (Luke 11:13) then I was going to ask until I received. I wasn't sure what to expect but I hoped my experience would be just like that of the New Testament believers in the book of Acts.

From that day on, I read every book I could find on how to receive the Holy Spirit. If someone said they received the Spirit while taking a shower, then I would hop in the shower and pray. If someone told me it happened to them while they were sitting outside by a rock, then I would go outside and sit by a rock and pray. I tried everything anyone suggested. I sat in a rocking chair praying. I laid face down on the floor begging. I asked others to pray for me, but nothing worked. I went to God in tears asking Him why He wouldn't baptize me in His Spirit, but all of heaven was silent. I couldn't figure out what sin I had committed, so I repented of everything from smoking to adultery. Nothing happened.

I had no idea that God was even then planning to answer my prayer through some dirty clothes and a trip to the local Laundromat.

21

DELIVERANCE

    One day the thought came into my mind that I should go to the Laundromat to wash clothes. The impression was so strong that I gathered my clothes and headed out. I found a Laundromat not far from my mom's apartment.
    I went inside, found a washer, dumped my clothes in along with the detergent, inserted the coins and pushed the start button. I then wandered over by the chairs and sat down next to a young man who looked familiar. I started up a conversation with him and discovered his name was Lee. As it turned out we had both graduated from Parkside High School and knew some of the same people. Lee went on to tell me that he was a Christian and that he helped to start the St. Mary's Charismatic meetings that I had attended just last Sunday. When he found out that I was a Christian he told me stories of people getting healed and delivered of demonic problems. As he unveiled the details of some of the stories of deliverance it struck a familiar chord in my heart. Some of the problems the people were struggling with sounded just like my own problems. He went on to explain that demons are called "evil spirits" in the Bible. They are usually invisible to humans because they operate in a different realm. They attach themselves to people attempting to work out (manifest) their nature. For example, a lying spirit causes people to lie, a spirit of depression causes people to be depressed and a spirit of suicide causes people to attempt suicide. Many people view these

manifestations as part of their personality or a psychological problem, but God's Word says they can be manifestations of demons.

As Lee spoke about deliverance, my mind conjured up images from my own past. At the age of six I had met some gypsies in Florida who taught me how to read palms and tell the future with cards. It seemed like harmless fun, yet from that moment on I began to have strange dreams at night that made me feel like I was in the very presence of some evil creature. My parents passed it off as a normal part of childhood, but to me it was very real. As a teenager I had advanced to using the Ouija Board, a demonic game sold in toy stores. It's a device that was designed to help people make contact with the spirit realm. Questions are asked and the Board responds by spelling out words or giving "Yes" and "No" answers. I seemed to have better "luck" at it than my friends. By the time I joined the army I was practicing astrology, hypnosis, ESP and witchcraft. I saw manifestations of supernatural power which served only to draw me deeper into the occult.

I later discovered that demons are like blood suckers that try to suck the very life out of people and they don't always leave when someone commits their life to Christ. Demons need to be exposed and then driven out. In the Bible the story is told about the people of Israel receiving the promised land from God. Yet even though it was theirs *technically,* they had to go in and drive out the inhabitants. So it is with people who have demons, the demons rarely leave on their own. They need to be driven out.

I knew what Lee was talking about when he spoke of people seeking power from demons. I was one of them. In our discussion, Lee briefly outlined the steps for deliverance and said he would be available later if I thought I needed help.

When I got home I called Lenore and told her of my conversation with Lee. Much to my surprise she believed in healings and deliverance too. She told me about some fascinating tapes on the subject of deliverance by an Englishman, Derek Prince. We decided to get together to listen to them. Several other people joined us.

On the first tape Derek told the story of how God led him into a deliverance ministry. When the tape was over we talked about what Derek said. Most of the group thought it was possible to have demonic problems today but didn't have any experience in it. We listened to one more tape before a few of people in our group had to leave. This demon thing sounded

Deliverance

a little too spooky for most of them. I continued until I had listened to all six tapes. Then I called Lee and set up a time to deal with demons that I now believed were at work in my own life.

When I arrived at Lee's house, he kissed his wife and children good night as we headed out the door. We were to meet with some other Christians in a house two doors down from Lee's. We climbed the stairs to an upper room where the deliverance was to take place. Lee left for awhile to pray in another room. He reappeared fifteen minutes later and said he was ready. There were four of us in that little room. We began with a time of confession of sins and prayed for the protection of everyone present. Lee felt it was important that I confess my involvement with the occult and prayerfully renounce those evil practices. I also had to make the decision to forgive anyone that I held anything against. Then Lee came over to me and laid his hand on my head and prayed to Jesus. When he was done praying, he changed his tone of voice and with authority began to come against any evil spirits.

"In the name of Jesus Christ, I command any evil spirit in this man to manifest yourself."

Nothing happened, so Lee tried again.

"Evil spirits in this man, I'm speaking to you and not to Denny. In the name of Jesus Christ, I command you to manifest yourself and come out of him."

As Lee continued I began to sense a small quivering deep inside. It kept growing in intensity until my whole body was shaking. Lee took this as a positive sign and continued.

"The Bible says that the demons tremble at the name of Jesus and I can see you demons trembling because you know you're going to have to leave as I command you to do so in Jesus' name. Evil spirit now controlling this man, what is your name?"

"Lust!" I heard my voice say. "And I'm not coming out."

"Oh yes you are." Lee retorted. "You have to come out because Jesus said so and it is in His name that I demand you to leave."

It took several minutes before the spirit gave in and left. But when it did I could feel it leave. It was as if I were a by-stander to this whole thing. I had no control over my body. As the first demon left, I sensed another one rise up in it's wake. This time I began to roar like a lion as I was taken over by a sense of rage.

"You spirit of violence, I command you to loose this man!"

No one in the room knew that I had struggled with a violent temper all my life. Now I understood why it seemed to possess me at times causing me to hurt other people.

One by one, the demons left but not without a fight. They each insisted that they had a right to be in my body because I had invited them in, either by my actions or by an actual invitation. As each demon left God showed me how they entered and what they drove me to do. But the last two really amazed me

A spirit took over my mouth and caused me to act like I was blowing smoke rings, a trick I had learned in my youth. As Lee commanded that spirit to leave, my whole face contorted and my jaw felt like it was trying to leave my face through the back of my neck. I thought I was going to choke to death as I struggled to breathe. I had no control over my body. Lee continued to command the demon to leave and when it did my desire for cigarettes also left. Somehow I knew I would never smoke another cigarette again. I discovered later that not all smokers have a demonic problem as I did. For some people it is just a bad habit that needs to be broken through discipline.

The last demon caused me to bark like a dog. As Lee tried to get it to leave my body, my mind raced back to my childhood and my fear of dogs. I remembered my mom saying that when she was pregnant with me she used to be chased by a barking dog in the downstairs apartment almost every day. She was terrified by that dog. I had been afraid of dogs all my life and I didn't know why, but the Lord revealed to me that a spirit of fear attached itself to me while I was still in my mother's womb. Therefore, my fear of dogs went beyond the realms of what was normal. I was being driven by a demon of fear related to dogs.

"Evil spirit in this man, I command you to tell me your name!"

"FEAR . . . and I have controlled him for a long time."

Lee commanded it to leave and as it left I felt a great peace settle over me. I sank to the floor exhausted and drenched. Lee came over and talked to me for a few minutes and then, laying his hands on me, prayed for me to be filled with the Holy Spirit. As Lee prayed, I began to praise God in a

Deliverance

different language that I had never learned. What a wonderful way to top off the evening.

As I left that upper room I was as different as the disciples were after Pentecost. This was what the Lord had in store for me in answer to my prayers. I never would have thought that the root to some of my problems were demonic in nature if it hadn't been for dirty clothes and a trip to a Laundromat. God truly works in mysterious ways!

22

WHAT REALLY HAPPENED?

I told everyone I could about my salvation and deliverance, but it sounded too bizarre for most people to accept. Many of my friends tried to convince me that I was stretching the truth. They presumed that things like this just didn't happen in this day and age.

I was told that demon possession simply did not occur in America. It only happened in primitive societies, like Haiti and Africa where people didn't know any better. I was challenged to rethink what really happened to me. Some suggested that I was influenced by the cassette tapes of Derek Prince and therefore I faked a deliverance based on what I had been taught. Other well meaning Christians offered the following insight:

"Many people would like to call their problems 'demons' because the cure is so much easier than having to discipline themselves to change behavior patterns. The mind plays funny tricks on us and our imaginations can become vivid enough that we think we experience things that we really didn't. Miracles like healing and speaking in tongues don't exist today because they ceased with the apostles, if they ever existed at all. Therefore, whatever you experienced, it was not deliverance."

From the Point to the Cross

This questioning of my experience really baffled me, especially since some of the people asking the questions were Christians who seemed to love the Lord. I was confused. Who should I listen to? Was I healed in Korea or was it just a dream? Did I really have demons cast out of me or did I fake the whole thing? Did I really speak in tongues or was it a counterfeit of Satan to confuse me? Was Jesus real? Did He really die on a cross and rise from the dead? Am I really forgiven? All of those questions seemed to have been answered by my experiences and what the Bible had to say. The experiences seemed real to me, but now I wasn't sure. I knew my desire for cigarettes was totally gone but was that just the power of suggestion?

I went back to the Bible and saw recorded instances of healings and deliverance's in the Gospels and the book of Acts. Then I remembered some older Christians telling me that God works differently in this dispensation of time. He no longer does healing miracles because that was only for the establishing of the early church. But could it be that those people were sincere but wrong? The Bible never says that miracles will cease and from where I was viewing life, it sure seemed like we needed miracles more now than ever.

In the midst of my confusion, a wonderful thing happened. I decided to go with the Bible and my experience and put aside all the comments of other people. Therefore, the day I made that decision I witnessed to anyone I could about how the Lord had set me free of evil spirits. I told people how I had been deceived by Satan to become involved in the occult, witchcraft, astrology, astral projection, ouija boards, mediums, and hypnosis. I believed that I knew things now that other people didn't know because I had once served the devil and now I served Jesus Christ. I went to bed that night praising God for a full day of trying to minister to others.

However, about 2:30 in the morning I woke up out of a sound sleep knowing someone was in the room with me. I sensed danger like I had so many times in Vietnam. I looked around the room but didn't see anything. I laid my head back on the pillow cautiously. Suddenly, something pounced on me and was trying to choke me. I was paralyzed from the tip of my toes to the hair on my head. I couldn't move. I was gasping for breath as I cried out in a whisper, "Jesus". As soon as I called on Jesus the thing on me jumped off. I could still sense it in the room so I started praying the Lord's Prayer and quoting any Bible verse I could think of. Suddenly it jumped back on me with renewed vigor. I called out to Jesus and it jumped off, just as it had before. Before it could attack again I kept saying the name of Jesus over and over.

"Jesus, I praise You. You are my Savior and my Deliverer. Blessed be Your name. Save me from this thing attacking me, Jesus."

It was as if I could almost see some evil being standing by the door watching me and waiting for another opportunity. But as I continued to call on Jesus, it left. When it was gone I got out of bed and turned on the lights to look for my Bible. I sat down in the living room with my Bible open, praising God for saving me from that thing, that I now believed was a demon. I had no idea at the time that I would face these kinds of battles in the spirit for the rest of my life on earth. My knowledge of the dark side would allow me to help many people be set free but would also cause me to undergo severe testing and continual attacks from demonic forces, whenever I got too close to their strongholds.

That night I laid my head on my open Bible and fell asleep calling on the wonderful name of Jesus. Now I was ready for Korea.

23

GROWING IN GRACE

On the way over to Korea I read a wonderful book entitled *Prison To Praise,* written by an Army chaplain, Merlin Carothers. I was encouraged by the book to pray specifically and then to praise God for the answer in advance. I put these lessons to work right away as I prayed that I could meet some other Christians to fellowship with in Korea.

During my first week back in Korea, God answered that prayer. I met another Christian brother and he invited me to the Christian Serviceman's Home in Seoul, the capitol of South Korea. The Home was run by an elderly couple that everyone called Mom & Pop Emerson. The Emerson's were Assembly of God missionaries.

I went to the Serviceman's Home and had a wonderful time. There were about fifty of us who enjoyed the family style meals Mom Emerson served. We had a service of singing and testimonies on Saturday night and a regular service on Sunday. However, our service on Sunday was preceded by attending the early service at the post chapel. The Emerson's wanted to maintain a good relationship with the Army Chaplains, so they supported chapel activities, even though many of the Chaplains didn't seem to accurately proclaim the truths of Scripture. The Emerson's eventually had me licensed to hold Bible studies in the Camp Red Cloud Chapel as a representative of the Assemblies of God.

From the Point to the Cross

Since I was excited about reaching my world for Christ, I witnessed to everyone I could. I made it a point to always pray over my food no matter who was around. This often led to opportunities to witness to someone or to meet another Christian. Very few of the men in my unit professed to be Christian, but I began to pray that God would change that.

One night I went to visit some men in another building, and as I walked into the room I smelled the sweet aroma of marijuana. I went up to the six men who were playing cards and began to share with them how Christ had changed my life. As I stood there witnessing to them, something I couldn't see attacked me. My legs began to buckle under as I felt intense pressure on my head and shoulders pushing me both down and away. My tongue felt like someone was tying it in a knot and I could barely breathe, as if I were being strangled. I knew in a moment that I was on Satan's turf and he was letting me know it in no uncertain terms.

"Jesus . . . Jesus . . . Jesus is Lord," I whispered with clenched teeth. Each time I said the name of Jesus I became stronger and the attack lessened. I continued until there was complete victory. With new freedom I once again told the men of the power of Jesus to change anyone's life, even dopers and potheads. They didn't fall down and repent and I wasn't sure if they could even hear me through the haze they were under. Yet as I walked away I rejoiced in the victory we have in Christ. Sharing about Jesus can't be stopped even by Satan.

As I prayed for the men in my unit I looked for any opportunity I could find to share God's truth. One of those opportunities came through the Army's ongoing battle against drugs. I discovered a film about drugs produced by "Teen Challenge". The film not only told the negative side effects of using drugs but it also shared the ministry of "Teen Challenge". I went to my commander and prayerfully asked if we could show it to the company and he agreed to do it as a training film. Everyone was required to attend the showing of the film and I invited Pop Emerson to come as a resource person for any questions. It was great day!

On another day, I was walking around the company area and singing happy songs of praise to the Lord when an officer came by. As I saluted him, he asked me why I was so happy and I simply responded, "JESUS!" He thought I was crazy, as did many of my co-workers, but it was the truth. I had something to sing about. I had found the answer to all my questions

Growing in Grace

in the person of Jesus Christ. Knowing Christ and helping others to know Him became my main purpose in life.

The Lord was gracious enough to use my awkward attempts to win people to Jesus. The first man I was able to win started off being my biggest enemy. As I continued to pray for him and share Christ with him, he eventually made the decision to invite Christ into his life. When others saw this man change, they wanted to know more. Soon there were several new Christians in my unit. On weekends we would go to the Christian Servicemen's Home for food, fellowship and fun. Once in awhile, we would even go out to a park in Seoul and through an interpreter, begin to witness to people. The Korean people were very interested in spiritual things and in a few minutes we would have a crowd of a hundred or more.

I loved Korea and the Korean people. I had many wonderful experiences during my one year tour in that far away land. One of those memorable events took place in the mountains, so far from civilization that there was no running water or electricity. It was a mission station called "The Jesus Abbey" and was run by a man of God named R. A. Torey. He lived with the people, dressed like them and ate what they ate. He had won the hearts of many. Another memorable moment was attending the largest church in the world, pastored by Paul Yongi Cho. The service was in Korean but it was great just to be there.

While in Korea, I asked Pop Emerson if he would baptize me. We used a Korean Church that had a good size "dunking pool" behind the pulpit. It marked the third time I was baptized but it was the only time I understood it as a believer in Christ.

I grew a lot in my understanding of what Christianity was all about during that year in Korea. I thought I had gained enough wisdom through my study of the Bible that I was ready for anything. I had no idea as I left for my next duty assignment at Ft. Meade, Maryland that I was walking into a trap of deception that I wouldn't even recognize.

24

LED ASTRAY

After my thirty days leave in Michigan I set out for Ft. Meade, Maryland. I was excited as I drove down the highway wondering what new adventures God would lead me into. I had a hot line to the Creator of the universe who often intervened to change the impossible in answer to the prayers of His people. Even as I drove, I reflected on one particular event that illustrated this point very well.

While I was on leave at home I had the opportunity of visiting an old girl friend named Brenda. She had been diagnosed with a diseased and failing kidney. A Christian friend of mine and I went to visit her in the hospital. We discovered that she was scheduled for an operation the following day. The surgery would involve the removal of her bad kidney. Before we left her room I asked if we could pray for her. Although she was not a praying person she agreed. My friend and I laid our hands on her (a Biblical concept taught in both Old and New Testaments) and we prayed for a healing of that bad kidney. Then we left. Several days later I received word that the doctors had done one final check on her kidney before operating and they discovered that the surgery was no longer needed. There was nothing wrong with her kidney. Praise God!

As I reflected on that event, I couldn't understand why God would chose to use me for such a miracle. I was an unworthy servant that didn't deserve any of God's blessings because of how I lived my life, yet God forgave me for everything. What an amazing thing from one so great. Forgiveness through Christ is the greatest miracle of all because it offers us a new beginning. Ft. Meade also offered me a new beginning. No longer would I be looking for the bars and dance halls so I could hustle girls. At Ft. Meade my first concern was how I could find a good church where other Christians gathered regularly to worship Jesus.

After visiting several churches, I discovered that I was a little too radical for a lot of the mainline churches. There had to be excitement, a loving fellowship, freedom of worship, evangelism and good Bible preaching for me to stick around. So when I first attended the "Local Church" of Washington D.C. founded by Witness Lee, a disciple of Watchman Nee, I thought I had arrived. On that first Sunday a couple invited me over for dinner and they were so kind that I came back the next week. That Sunday another couple invited me over for dinner. I wondered how they coordinated this but never did find out. On my next visit some of the young single guys invited me over for dinner. Before I left they had invited me to spend the next week-end with them.

On that Saturday almost the whole congregation gathered at the church building for spring cleaning. We started with a devotion on servant hood and then with glad hearts attacked the dirty toilets, floors, sinks and rooms. I never knew cleaning could be so much fun. Later that day we played touch football and then passed out Christian pamphlets on the streets of Washington D.C. We started the next day by "Pray-Reading The Word". This involved reading a passage of Scripture and then praying it. Let me illustrate by using the first verse of the twenty-third Psalm:

"The Lord is My Shepherd I shall not want."

"Jesus, You are my Shepherd . . . When You are my Shepherd I won't lack anything because You are leading and guiding me. Thank You, Jesus."

The Sunday service at the Local Church of Washington, D.C. was filled with excitement and joy. They had created their own songbook that had a lot of popular tunes but with Christian words substituted for the original ones. After each song, different people would stand up and tell which word or phrase of the song ministered to them. It was a wonderful way to focus on the great truths found in the songs.

Led Astray

Nevertheless, as the months went by something seemed wrong. I couldn't put my finger on it but I felt something just wasn't right. It wasn't until several years later that I discovered that some well known authorities believed that the "Local Church" was a cult. Personally, I never met a more committed, loving group of people that were so excited about their faith. But it didn't feel right for me, so I left.

As I was being weaned away from the Local Church I found a charismatic church that was just in the developmental stages. It was in Laurel, Maryland, just outside the gate of Ft. Meade. There was one couple, Jack and Jean Coleman, that I became especially fond of. Jack was one of the leaders (elders) of the church. The senior pastor was a young man half Jack's age. Jack seemed wiser and more mature in his faith than the senior pastor, so it seemed a little awkward.

A form of discipleship, known as shepherding, was a BIG issue in this young church. Everyone had to be submitted to someone else out of the fear that we would miss God's leading and direction. I submitted to Victor, an under-shepherd of the senior pastor. We were part of a world-wide shepherding movement led by five men in Florida: Derek Prince, Charles Simpson, Don Basham, Ern Baxter, and the head man, Bob Mumford. We felt we had to submit to our leaders who were God's chosen vessels. This included our finances, dating life, goals, time, and everything else. I went along with it for awhile but it didn't seem right. Jack and Jean were struggling with it too. We often met together to pray and visit. They were great, but the tension in the church for the three of us was getting to be too much. I felt like I was being led astray and knew that somehow I had to find God's truth and His will for my life.

25

IS ANYONE ALWAYS RIGHT?

Several positive things happened to me while I was attending the shepherding Church in Laurel, Maryland. One bright spot was a young college student named Margy. She attended the same church I did and we just hit it off right away. After dating for several months, I asked her to marry me and she said "Yes." But her father said "No!" He didn't think I had anything to offer Margy. He was a successful businessman and from where he stood, my future looked pretty dim. He pointed to my lack of skills and said I had no way to earn a living so I could support a family. Another big issue with him was the fact that I currently had no money saved for the future. I tried to tell him that Margy and I were trusting God to take care of us but to him that sounded like foolishness. Our relationship fizzled out after that and Margy later married a dentist.

I continued to attend the same Church but the longer I went the more uncomfortable I felt. The final straw for me came when I was getting ready to get out of the Army. The leaders at the church said I needed to find a job in the area, get married and settle down in Laurel. However, as I went job hunting all the doors of opportunity closed in my face. My relationship with Margy had failed because her parents would not give us their blessing, so I couldn't see any reason to stay in the area. One day I was walking through a mall when I spotted Jack and Jean. They had recently left the shepherding church. We engaged in small talk for a few minutes and then we focused in on my problem. Right there in the mall Jack asked me a very important question that would change the whole direction of my life.

"What do you WANT to do, if you could do anything?"

I knew in an instant what my answer would be, "Go to Bible college."

"Then why don't you go?" Jack responded. "Maybe God put that desire on your heart for a reason."

The only reason I could think of for not going was that the leaders told me not to. Later that day I went over to Jack and Jean's home and they gave me a flyer on Elim Bible Institute, which they recommended very highly. In a matter of only a few days I had applied and was accepted. The following Sunday I tried to explain to the shepherding church how God had led me to leave for Bible college. After I sat down several of the leading elders stood up and rebuked me, saying I was off on my own without God's blessing. One of the leaders said that if he needed to know God's will all he had to do was to go to his under-shepherd and ask him. As I sat there listening to these men I became even more convinced that I was right and they were wrong. I couldn't wait to get out from underneath that bondage.

I came to the conclusion, that no person (other than God) is always right 100% of the time: no pastor, no teacher, no church. What so often happens is that we find someone we respect and assume that because they were right on one thing, they must be right on everything. I had done that with Derek Prince. I assumed that since he was right about deliverance then he must also be right about everything else - - including shepherding. I was wrong! No one but God is always right. Therefore, only God can be trusted to direct our lives.

During my final week in the area I attended a seminar on faith, with an emphasis on healing. It was being led by C.J. Mahaney, who along with Larry Tomzack had started an exciting weekly meeting called TAG (Take and Give). Both men were dynamic speakers and wonderful teachers of the Bible. At the seminar C.J. taught how important faith is for releasing the power of God. By the time the seminar was over I was pumped full of faith.

I was discharged from the Army on August 24, 1975. As I drove out of town I left with the rebuke of the shepherding church and the blessing of my adopted spiritual parents, Jack and Jean Coleman. I had purchased some tapes on faith by C.J. Mahaney that I listened to as I drove toward

Is Anyone Always Right?

Michigan. When I came to the Allegheny Mountains in Pennsylvania I pulled off the highway at a scenic rest area. I walked over to the edge of the cliff and glanced down at the beautiful canyon below, took my glasses off and dropped them on the ground and stomped on them.

"Satan, as Jesus crushed your head under His feet when He died on the cross, I now crush these glasses and the curse of farsightedness. Heavenly Father, I claim healing for my eyes now by faith in Jesus Christ and the promises of Your Word. By His stripes I'm healed! Praise God!"

I bent over and picked up my mangled glasses and threw them into the canyon. "Take that, Satan. You can have my glasses because I won't be needing them anymore."

I walked back to my car and drove away, straining my eyes to see the signs ahead and shouting for all to hear, "BY HIS STRIPES I'M HEALED!"

26

BIBLE COLLEGE

I was excited about Bible college and the opportunity to study the Bible under gifted teachers. Elim Bible Institute was located in Lima, New York, just south of Rochester. They had been training charismatic leaders for ministry and mission for many years. It is a great school with a good reputation. When I arrived I got settled in my dorm room and then walked around the campus. While walking I met a young man named Ron Griffin who just happened to be from Jackson, Michigan. We had never met each other even though we were both raised in the same town.

Ron and I were very much alike. Ron was a radical Christian with a hunger to know God and study His Word. It was that desire that brought him to Bible college. We hit it off so well together that it seemed like we had known each other all our lives. During those Bible college days Ron and I became the best of friends.

One of the things Ron taught me was the fine art of door-to-door evangelism. I had done a lot of evangelism through friendships and even walking up to strangers on the street, but going door-to-door seemed like invading someone's private turf. However, after several months of being spoon-fed the Word of God I was chomping at the bit to reach out in some type of ministry, so Ron and I attacked a nearby town going from house to house sharing what Jesus had done in our lives. We had a great time even though only about 10% of the people would talk to us. Many of them had probably had bad experiences with Jehovah Witnesses, Mormons, or other cult groups and therefore slammed the door in our face too. They probably thought they would discourage us but it had just the opposite effect. Ron and I became radical in our witnessing attempts and shared with others at the college what we were doing. As we told others, they wanted in on the action too and soon we had a team of about fifteen people going out. We went to homes, apartments, bars, restaurants, colleges, and any other place we could get an audience. Many people were won to the Lord during those ventures. However, it always bothered me that we couldn't do a better job of following up on them. Because of my own experience I knew how important it was to teach new Christians the basics of the faith. But what were those basics? All Christians certainly needed to learn how to study the Bible, how to pray, the importance of Christian fellowship, and tips on witnessing. Interestingly, the Bible doesn't list any of those as the place to start with new believers. Hebrews 6: 1-2 lists seven doctrines that are the foundation blocks for solid Christians.

"Therefore, let us leave the elementary teachings about Christ and go on to maturity, not laying again the foundation of repentance from acts that lead to death, and of faith in God, instruction about baptisms, the laying on of hands, the resurrection of the dead, and eternal judgment."

Our teams believed in the power of God to do miracles. Gary Lizardo and I were often very outspoken when it came to discussions about divine healing. Gary was from Niagara Falls and just seemed to move in power. People were often slain in the Spirit when Gary prayed for them. That didn't happen very often with me. Yet I did see many people healed anyway. I made it a habit to pray for anyone who needed healing and often saw immediate results, but in the process I became prideful. I have since learned that pride is one of the biggest reasons God has to limit the giving of His power to people. Once God starts to use us in miracles we forget where the power comes from and become possessive of it, as if in some way we generated it by ourselves (Acts 3:12-16). I have first hand knowledge of that because it happened to me, but God knew just what to do to humble me.

It happened one day in a chapel service. As students, we were required to attend chapel three to four times a week. One day while everyone had their eyes closed worshipping God, it seemed like God grabbed me by both shoulders and lifted me up in the air and whispered in my ear a staggering question,

"Do you think you know all there is to know about healing?"

I slithered down into the pew, ashamed of my arrogance. I wept before the Lord that day and asked for His forgiveness. In that moment, I had gained a new perspective on healing. Only God knew all the answers. I was reminded of my own situation with my eyes. I still wasn't able to read the print on the blackboards in my classes. For over a year I continued to confess that I'd been healed according to Isaiah 53:5 & 6 - - but I never saw the manifestation of it. When it came time to renew my driver's license I couldn't see to pass the test and had to break down and buy some glasses. I learned that healing doesn't always work just because we want it, claim it and maintain a good confession. Divine healing comes only from God. He may use people whom He has gifted for that ministry but He is always the one behind the actual miracles.

I must have had some other rough edges too because people frequently came up to me apologizing for hating me. When I would inquire what I had done, they often responded by saying that I bugged them by acting happy and singing all the time. I took God's Word literally when He said we should rejoice always (Philippians 4:4). I put it into practice and people got mad at me for it. It did wonders for me but it had just the opposite effect on other people. For many people life was tough and rejoicing didn't come easy. Therefore, it seemed strange to them to see someone like me praising God most of the time. I was excited about serving the Lord and wanted to obey Him in all things. It was at about that time that a great opportunity came my way to see if I really did want to obey God all the way.

27

HEARING GOD

It was always difficult to find a place to pray alone at Elim. Almost all of the students were excited about the Lord and praying daily was just something excited Christians do. Two of my favorite places to pray at Elim were outside on the ball field at night and in the furnace room of my dorm. The furnace room was warm and I found that the noise of the furnace helped to drown out my voice - - at least I hoped no one actually heard me. During those times of prayer with the Lord I found myself falling more in love with Jesus every day. At times I was so anxious to be alone with the Lord that I couldn't wait to get into that furnace room. I remember one night being surrounded by students and yet longing to be with Jesus. We had to be in attendance at some meetings but during one of the breaks I rushed into a phone booth, closed the door, and pretended to dial a number. For the next five minutes I talked with God on my hotline to heaven (Jer 33:3).

One day about a dozen of us were sitting around in the sanctuary discussing the leading of the Lord in our lives. We were asked to explain where we felt God was leading us. Most of the group said, "Oh, I'm not sure right now. I'm just waiting to hear from God. I'll go where He leads." There were a few who were a little more specific by saying, "I feel like God is leading me into youth work." But when it came my turn I blew everyone

away with a list of ten things I felt God was leading me to accomplish in my life.
1. Become a military Chaplain
2. Get married and start a family
3. Work as an assistant pastor
4. Become a full-time pastor
5. Start a church
6. Get a Bachelors, Masters, and Doctorate Degrees
7. Preach in Australia
8. Write some books
9. Teach at the college level
10. Be a missionary

When people heard my list they thought I was being very arrogant and presumptuous. I explained to them that the Bible said that God would give us the desires of our heart (Psalm 37:4) and I was just foolish enough to believe it. I believed that God was the one who put those desires in my heart to begin with because I constantly prayed for His will to be done in my life. Furthermore, for me to accomplish any of those things would require His divine intervention.

It has always amazed me that people don't seem to have dreams that they prayerfully seek after. Yet God has often used the dreams of His people to accomplish great things. Think of the dreams of Daniel, Joseph, David, or the Apostle Paul. Today many people talk about setting goals, but goals are just another way of trying to accomplish your dreams. For every dream or goal there are always hoops we have to jump through. When God gives us a dream there is always something we have to do to see it happen. God does His part but only when we do our part. It is a team effort, but God controls the stop watch. It happens in His time not when we want it.

Amazingly His divine intervention often comes at unexpected times during normal routine events that turn into major crossroads in life. Such was the case one day during a normal chapel service. In Bible college we dealt with a lot of guilt. The college always invited in special speakers from all over the world who challenged us to join their mission organizations. These challenges left us confused because they all sounded good. But one day I heard a challenge that I couldn't walk away from.

Hearing God

Dave Bret represented a mission group called Youth With A Mission (YWAM). Dave was recruiting workers for a short term mission trip to Scotland in the summer of 1976. As he spoke, his words touched my heart and I knew God wanted me involved. I heard no voice other than Dave Bret's but it was like God was calling me to Scotland. I picked up the packet of information after the meeting and filled it out that night. The next day I prayerfully put it in the mail and committed the whole thing to God. It took about six weeks to get a reply saying that I was accepted. However, I would need a passport and a plane ticket. YWAM is called a "faith mission" made up of volunteers who receive no monetary reimbursement for their labor. They believe that if God called you to work for Him, then He would provide for you. One of their frequently quoted sayings puts it this way, "Where God guides - - He provides."

As a full-time student I had no income to purchase a plane ticket so I had to wait on God to provide for that part of the trip. But I could go ahead and get a passport. I went down to apply at the government office but I didn't have my birth certificate, so I couldn't go through the processing. When I got back to the dorm I went through everything I had but could not find my birth certificate. I called my mom in Michigan and asked her to send me a copy but she didn't have one either. She told me to call Lansing, Michigan where all the records were kept. I called the Lansing office but they didn't have one, so I gave up. It seemed to me that God didn't want me to go to Scotland with YWAM, at least not in the summer of 1976. Therefore, as summer approached I made plans to live on a nearby farm with Jim Carlson and his family. I got a job making prefabricated houses. It looked like my plans for the summer were all set in place. However, God was setting me up for a miracle so that I would know beyond a shadow of a doubt that I was in His perfect will.

28

YOUTH WITH A MISSION (Y.W.A.M.)

One Saturday morning I woke up early with a strange thought in my mind. I felt I should go to the closet and look in a certain bag for my birth certificate. The idea seemed stupid to me since I had already searched through everything I owned several times without seeing it. Still the thought persisted.

"God, are You trying to tell me something?" I prayed as I climbed out of bed. I went to the closet and found the bag I pictured in my mind. I pulled it out of the closet and looked inside. There on top of everything else was my birth certificate. I grabbed it and held it up in amazement.

"Lord, does this mean You want me to go to Scotland with YWAM?"

I knew the answer even before the words were out of my mouth.

"Lord, You know my situation. I don't have the money to get there, so I need to rely on You to provide it for me. If You supply it I'll go, but somehow You will need to help me get a passport in time and a plane ticket." I thought for a minute and then added, "Lord, there is one other problem, my new job. I have been telling everyone there about You and if I just go up to the boss and tell him I can't work any more than two weeks, they are going to think I'm crazy. Somehow help me to get out of that situation without disgracing You or me. All this is in Your hands. Thanks Lord."

The passport office was closed on Saturday, so I returned on Monday with all the proper forms in hand. The woman behind the counter informed me that passports usually take about six weeks to two months. I told her I needed it in one week. She thought I was crazy to even submit the paper work but I did anyway. Then I made a reservation for a flight into Glasgow, Scotland and tried to explain to the ticket agent that I would pay when I arrived at the airport. I was trusting God for the money but I couldn't tell her that.

As the week passed I began to receive a trickle of extra money that I wasn't expecting. It came from different sources and in different ways. One check was from my insurance company that just had a change in policy which meant a refund. Several people who owed me money had decided to send it, and some other friends felt impressed for some reason to send me some money. One night I attended a church I had never been to and at the end of the service several people came up and gave me money saying they felt God wanted them to do that. With each little bit of money that came in my faith grew.

On Friday of that week about one hour before the whistle blew all the workers were called into the lunch room for a special meeting with the boss. He said he didn't understand what was going on with the market. Usually the summer months were very busy, but this year he said he would have to lay some of us off until the slump was over. He said that if we had a pink slip in with our check for the week that we were laid off until further notice.

I opened my envelope and saw my pink slip behind my check. "Praise God!" I shouted. I was probably the only employee that reacted to that pink slip by praising God. But then no one but the Lord and I knew that I had prayed for just such an event to happen. I jumped in my car and praised God all the way home.

When I arrived at home I opened my mail only to discover that I was now the proud owner of a new, official American passport. That sent me off on another round of praises to the Lord.

Over the next few days all the pieces of the puzzle fell into place, even though I didn't have all the money until about two hours before the plane was to take off. God is never late but He sure takes His time about coming to our rescue. Maybe that's why some say that He is the "three-mile-an-hour-God". When I got on the plane a man sat next to me and during the course of our brief time together pulled out a twenty dollar bill and gave it to me. That would be the extent of my spending money.

Youth With A Mission (Y. W. A. M.)

Once in Scotland I boarded a bus and headed for YWAM headquarters in Edinburgh.

I arrived safely several hours later. Our training consisted of classes during the day and short evangelistic excursions at least once every 72 hours. This went on for about two weeks. We then divided into small teams and each team set up a base in a different town. I was sent to Jedbourgh and put in charge of that team of about 10 people. We lived in an Episcopal Church and tried to assist the local pastors. Our job was to win people to Christ any way we could without being obnoxious.

We had the freedom to try anything. We held open air meetings in the park, went door-to-door, attempted street evangelism, and utilized revival techniques in the local churches. Since I loved evangelism I was having a ball, but no one responded to our efforts. Yet we had to continue going out every day whether they responded or not. I soon discovered that even evangelism can be tough work. Eventually, I came to the point that I dreaded it. After all, what's the use if no one responds?

One day I handed a Gospel tract to a store owner who began yelling at me to get out of his country.

"Get out of my store and out of my country. You Americans have more problems than we do, so go preach to your own people. You have no right here. GET OUT!" Then he pushed me right out of his store.

I reflected on that man's comment the rest of the day and into the night. He had a point, yet God had led me to Scotland. I couldn't understand why we weren't seeing any results. Why weren't any lives being changed? I didn't have the answer to that question but I knew that God did. The rest of the team left for a weekend retreat but I stayed behind alone to fast and pray.

I often pace when I pray to the Lord. As I was praying and moving about the church I noticed some old books on a window ledge. I went over to them and found one that sounded interesting: *The Revival We Need* by Oswald J. Smith.

The book told the story of a pastor who wanted to see revival in his church. He studied every book on the subject and read biographies of all the great saints of the church. He discovered that there were certain elements in all the revivals of history. The main three elements were prayer, open confession of sin, and desire (P-O-D). Revival always seems to begin with God placing the desire for revival on someone's heart. That desire then takes them into their prayer closet. While in prayer they sense the holiness of God and begin to repent for their own sin and the sin of others, asking God to have mercy.

Oswald J. Smith's desire led him to spend long hours in prayer to God. During those times he became convicted of sins he wasn't even aware he had committed. Yet those very sins he felt had held back the hand of God and the work of the Holy Spirit. From his own experience Mr. Smith suggested that those seeking revival needed to cleanse their own heart first. As an aid for this heart searching he listed some questions that should be asked:

1. Is there hatred, spite or malice in my heart?
2. Do I need to forgive anyone?
3. Does wrath and anger hold me in its grip?
4. Am I jealous or envious of anyone else?
5. Am I impatient with others and easily irritated?
6. Do I get offended easily?
7. Is there pride in my heart?
8. Have I been dishonest in my dealings with others?
9. Have I been slandering or gossiping about others?
10. Am I looking for flaws in others to criticize?
11. Have I robbed God in time or money?
12. Am I worldly and enjoying the sinful pleasures of the world?
13. Do I take things that don't belong to me?
14. Do I harbor a spirit of bitterness?
15. Is my life filled with frivolity?
16. Do I treat the things of God lightly?
17. Have I wronged anyone and failed to make restitution?
18. Am I worried or anxious and not trusting God?
19. Is my mind filled with impure or lustful thoughts?
20. Do I tell the truth or too often exaggerate?
21. Do I believe the promises in God's Word ?
22. Am I guilty of the sin of unbelief?
23. Have I committed the sin of prayerlessness?
24. Have I neglected God's Word?
25. Have I been ashamed to confess Christ openly?
26. Have I failed to have compassion for the lost?

Youth With A Mission (Y. W. A. M.)

As I studied the list of questions I had two reactions. My first impulse was to say everybody was guilty of these at some time, so why should I repent of them? My second reaction was to see that my actions had grieved the heart of God and I fell on my face in repentance.

I began to confess the sins I was reminded of from Mr. Smith's list. I also thought of other things I had done that seemed wrong so I confessed those too. Lying prostrate on the floor with my head buried in the rug I began to weep for myself and then for the lost people of Jedbourgh. I asked the Holy Spirit to intercede in prayer through me. The power of God flooded the room and I began to groan deep within. I couldn't speak any words at all. All I could do was moan and weep. I felt such compassion for the lost people of Jedbourgh that I couldn't even describe it. I finally understood in a deeper way Romans 8:26:

"The Spirit helps us in our weakness. We do not know what we ought to pray, but the Spirit Himself intercedes for us with groans that words cannot express."

This deep and special type of prayer occurred several times over that weekend. Each time it was accompanied by an awesome awareness of the presence of God. By the time the team arrived I was ready to hit the streets and share with people what Jesus could do.

When we did go back out, for the first time people responded. Healings occurred, people were open to the Gospel and some even committed their lives to Christ. I had learned a valuable lesson about evangelism: Before we go out to talk to people about God, we should talk to God about the people we hope to encounter. Without prayer there can be no revival or evangelism.

When my six weeks were up I decided to change my flight plans to make it easier on the YWAM team, so I switched the place of my departure to one closer to our base of operation. While that made a lot of sense to me, I forgot to ask God what He thought about it. It was simply a matter of canceling my flight from New York City to Rochester and applying credit to my new flight from Edinburgh to Glasgow. I kept thinking someone would hand me money at the last minute before I got on the flight, but it never happened. I boarded the plane for the United States and had to call for help when I touched down in New York or be stranded there forever. Somehow my lesson on prayer didn't sink in when it applied to other aspects of life, only with reference to revival. But fortunately, God hadn't given up on me yet.

When I arrived at home I received a call from the place where I had worked before leaving for Scotland. They wanted everyone to return to work because things were finally picking up. The leaders of that company had no idea that God was involved in the ups and downs of their business during the summer of 1976. That was a secret only the Lord and I knew. What a mighty God we serve!

29

FAILURE

Before I left for Scotland in June, I had been invited to attend one of the churches in Rochester. It turned out to be a large non-denominational Church with a lot of young women and very few men. In their desperation to find Christian men the ladies of that church decided to form a prayer group with the express purpose of praying for eligible young Christian bachelors to come to that church.

I attended an evening service and afterwards had the opportunity of meeting several of those radical young women. I was especially attracted to the ring leader of the group. She worked in one of the local hospitals as a nurse and was a vibrant Christian with a heart for doing God's will. Upon hearing of her desire to find a Christian husband and noticing how attractive she was, I returned to my dorm and prayed to the Lord about her becoming my wife. For several days I prayed earnestly that God would give her to me as a wife. I even asked the Lord to somehow bring her to the school I was attending. After a week or so, I got bogged down in my studies and forgot about her. But God didn't.

When the fall semester started that nurse was a student at my Bible college. I didn't know how to react. We didn't talk much and I didn't think she even knew who I was, but I watched her all the time wondering if she could be the one God had for me. I had heard different teachings on the subject of finding a marriage partner. Some Christians taught that God had only one person in the world selected for us and we needed to wait until He brought the two of us together. Those adhering to this view often felt that even standing in the lunch line could be that divine moment of their encounter with that special someone. Therefore, they had to be on the lookout just in case. Since many of the students believed in this teaching it made the meal line very interesting. There were other Christian teachers who believed that we could marry anyone we wanted to. They taught that it was up to us to make that decision since God gave us a brain and the freedom to make choices.

At that point in my life, I didn't know how it worked but I did know I wanted God's best. I just wasn't sure if the nurse was the right person for me. I often wondered if I had prayed wrongly. I was confused, so I held back and observed from a distance.

As the semester came to an end an unexpected voice from by past came on the scene. I began receiving frequent long distance phone calls from Connie, Kescia's mother. She often ended up crying over the phone as she tried to explain how tough things were for her and Kescia. The conversation would usually include Connie telling me that I had more than just a financial obligation to fulfill through child support. It was obvious that Kescia needed a dad and Connie needed a husband, but I had some real doubts about the whole thing. I wanted to do what was right, but it didn't seem like Connie and I were right for each other. We had nothing in common except Kescia. Our lifestyles were totally different.

To make matters worse, Connie began calling different members of the faculty to tell them her plight. This resulted in many counseling sessions with the Dean of Students, the Dean of Men, the Vice-President of the college, and various teachers who wanted to offer helpful advice. I sought God day after day, but all of heaven seemed silent. Some of the people I admired at the school said I was under a Biblical mandate to marry her. Others said that what took place in my life before Jesus was forgiven. Several people on the staff urged me not to marry her, while others told me I had no choice. I wasn't sure what to do.

In the midst of all the confusion there was only one thing of which I was sure. I knew there was a little five year old girl by the name of Kescia who needed a father. All my life I'd had a love for children and hoped to have a family of my own someday. Furthermore, I knew that I served a God of miracles. I reasoned that if God could change my life, then surely He could

Failure

change Connie. I felt I needed to make right my wrong. I had to go back. My decision was made.

The day I was scheduled to leave I went into the chapel to say good-bye to some friends and ran into the nurse I had prayed for. She was being counseled by several other students because she too was in a state of confusion. She looked at me and asked a question I would never forget.

"Denny, I'm not sure what I'm doing here. I felt led of the Lord to leave my job and come here to school but now I'm not sure why. Do you have any insight into why I might be here?"

I was stunned. I was just getting ready to get into my car and drive off into the sunset to marry Connie. Yet here before me sat a beautiful godly young woman asking if I knew why she was attending the very school I had prayed God would bring her to so that we could get acquainted and eventually marry. I was so in awe over the situation that I turned and ran out of the chapel. I jumped into my car and drove away not knowing what else to do since plans had already been made to marry Connie.

I returned to Michigan and without any courtship I married Connie within the week. Connie and I were legally husband and wife, but our lifestyles and priorities were worlds apart. On that first night of our honeymoon Connie told me she hated me and wanted a divorce. She couldn't believe that I was any different from when I used to hustle women in bars. In her eyes I would always be a low life scumbag. There was no miracle for us. Hatred and bitterness were too strong. Forgiveness would not be granted. The hurts were too deep. We managed to stay together for several months but it was rocky the whole time. After a three month separation we tried again. I had this weird notion that if Connie could get pregnant and discover that I wouldn't leave her that maybe things would be better between us. Perhaps that could bring about a healing. I was wrong.

When Connie got pregnant it drove us further apart. She hated me even more for getting her pregnant again. We fought constantly. I was there during the delivery of a baby girl whom we named Glorianna. However, after months of constant fighting and disagreements, we soon joined the ranks of those classified as divorced. I had failed. Since I was the one to leave, Connie blamed me for destroying her life and after awhile, I began to agree with her. Perhaps if I had done something different a miracle would have happened, or if I had been a better Christian things wouldn't have turned out as they did. But it did happen and there was no going back, I still loved Kescia and Glori, but I couldn't live with their mother.

As anyone knows who has been through a divorce, it is a very emotional time. A divorce not only divides a husband and wife, but it causes a ripple effect of separation that stretches to the grandparents, aunts, uncles, cousins, and even friends. Families who at one time went to Church together, suddenly no longer feel comfortable in that same Church. They often change to new restaurants, stores, and towns that don't remind them of their former spouse. Then there are all the legal proceedings including; appointments with lawyers, rulings by Friend of the Court on custody and support of the children, and legal confrontations with each other over who gets what.

Yet even after the divorce was final, the fights still didn't end. There were more battles with Connie on the phone, in letters, and in court. Connie tried to turn everyone against me as part of her battle plan. Yet her parents, who are good Christian people, never turned against me. They have, even to this day, treated me with kindness, understanding, and respect. I admire them for that.

At the time of the divorce I only knew how depressed I felt. I prayed frequently that God would just take me home to heaven to be with Him. I didn't deserve to live. I had hurt too many people. I was a failure as a father for Kescia and Glori and I had failed as a husband. I knew the Bible said that God hated divorce so I assumed that meant He hated me. It seemed like I had failed everyone in my life, including God. I wasn't sure about the future anymore. I had no sense of direction. I wondered how God could ever use me now? I felt rejected by God, the church, and my friends.

I saw myself as a man without hope. I could never go back to my old way of life because of my Christian convictions. Yet I couldn't seem to move forward toward my goals either. I was stuck in neutral and feeling worthless. I felt condemned reading the Bible and being around Christian people. Even praying was difficult. I wanted to die but I knew suicide was wrong. It seemed as if no one understood. Life was a daily struggle. I was defeated. Satan had won.

30

KAREN

Four things helped to pull me out of the depression I was in. The first was a visit from Paul Johannson, one of the deans at Elim Bible Institute. His visit was an act of mercy. Without any condemnation or taking sides he listened and then offered words of advice and comfort. Before he left we prayed together.

The second helpful thing was a degree program that I was involved in at Spring Arbor College in Michigan. I was working on a Bachelor of Arts degree in psychology. Being a very goal oriented person, I had to finish what I had started. It gave me the incentive I needed to go on.

The third was a singles support group that met every week. It was made up of mostly divorced people although there were a few widows in the group. The forth was a young woman named Karen, who was a student at Spring Arbor College majoring in Elementary Education. She was cheerful, sensitive, intelligent, caring, and attractive. Most important, she was also a committed Christian. She had a bubbly personality and I liked her as a person, but the thing that really impressed me was her heart for God. We'd often talk of spiritual things and in the process developed a trusting friendship. Karen and I knew each other for over a year before we ever went out on a date.

When we did start dating it just seemed like we hit it off right from the start. During one school break, she invited me to meet her parents and her only brother, Jeff. Her parents were very friendly and easy to talk to. Jeff had just returned from his first semester at the Air Force Academy in Colorado. He hoped to be either a doctor or a jet fighter pilot. He asked me a lot of questions about my experiences in Vietnam. When it was time for me to go, it seemed like my first visit with Karen's family was a success. I had passed the initial family inspection.

On New Years Eve Karen wanted me to meet one of her best friends, Fran King. Fran was married to Peter King, a neat Christian who hoped to go into the ministry someday. We had a great time together ushering in the New Year. But when it was time to leave it was snowing so badly that we called Karen's parents and spent the night with the King's. Fran was a nervous wreck, thinking I was going to seduce or rape her friend in the living room. Therefore, Fran insisted that Karen sleep on a cot in the kitchen. It was on that cot in the kitchen that Karen and I kissed for the first time (Honestly Fran - - that's all that happened!).

When school resumed, Karen and I started seeing each other more frequently. Since I was a full-time student during the day and worked third shift at a local factory, Karen worried about my poor eating habits. Therefore, she started cooking dinner for me every night so that I would at least eat one good meal a day. Karen had completed her college classes so she was free to substitute in the day time and help me at night, not only with dinner but also with my studies. We had the kind of relationship that allowed us to talk freely about almost everything. We spent a lot of time exploring our religious background because of the important part it had played in each of our lives.

Karen was raised in the Lutheran Church and attended Lutheran schools until the ninth grade. She had read the Bible, gone through the Lutheran catechism, and even joined the church. But it seemed as if something was missing in her life. She asked everyone she looked up to spiritually and they all consoled her by saying that she had all there was. When she was fourteen she attended a church camp. During that camp she met a pastor who said that he had pastored for many years but had only been a Christian for a couple of years. He explained that it is possible to know a lot of facts about Christ without really knowing Him personally. He encouraged her to pray and invite Christ into her life and to allow Jesus to live His life through her. Karen found a place to be alone on the beach and prayed for Jesus to come into her life. That prayer changed her life. Later, she started attending a charismatic church that was affiliated with Elim Fellowship. In that church she received the baptism of the Holy Spirit.

Karen and I continued to date, but our dates were not the normal run of the mill dates. We spent some of those dates as teachers of retarded adults. On other nights we were youth directors at a small United Methodist Church in Somer Set Center.

In the meantime, Karen and I had both already applied to different graduate schools without discussing it with each other. Karen's first choice was to go on for a Master's Degree in deaf education at Ball State University in Muncie, Indiana. My first choice was to pursue a Master's Degree in psychology and pastoral care at Anderson School of Theology in Anderson, Indiana. The schools were only about 25 miles apart.

By the time we received our letters of acceptance we were in love with each other and had decided that we wanted to spend the rest of our lives together as husband and wife. How special God is to have worked out the logistics of schools ahead of time!

Karen invited her parents to Spring Arbor the following Saturday and we made plans to fix them an unforgettable meal. I had only met Karen's parents on one occasion so I was a little apprehensive to ask them for their daughter's hand in marriage.

After a delicious meal we drove over to the church where Karen and I had been working as youth directors. At some point on that journey, I began to tell them about my past. I felt they had a right to know everything since I was about to ask for their permission to marry Karen. I also told them of my future plans to pursue a career in the ministry and that I wouldn't be able to provide great riches for their daughter. I spoke of the past, the present and the future, and I told them of my love for Karen. Then I popped the question to Karen's dad.

"Sir, I know I don't deserve a good woman like Karen after the kind of life I have lived but I love her with all my heart and would like your permission to marry her."

There was silence in the car yet I thought for sure everyone could hear the pounding of my heart as I waited for her father's answer. I noticed her parents glancing at each other before her dad broke the silence.

"It took a lot of guts to share all of that, Den."

"Sir, I believe you needed to know my background before giving your consent."

"Den, you have our permission."

"Praise God!"

At that point we all loosened up and began to talk at the same time. Karen's mom broke into the conversation and said something that I will never forget.

"We were looking at the size of your church even before you talked to us about marriage because Dad had said on the first day that he met you, Den, that you were the one Karen would marry. So we have been expecting this news."

The full revelation of that statement didn't hit me until after the wedding ceremony was over and Karen and I piled into her little blue Grèmlin to head out on our honeymoon. God was giving me another chance. I had once despaired of even life itself, but even through my failures God had worked out the details to bless my life through Karen.

31

GETTING IN

We spent the first week of our honeymoon leisurely touring Canada. The second week, however, held a very different agenda. Our mission was to find a place to live.

We traveled to Indiana where our schools were located and began apartment hunting. Most of the places within our budget were rundown and cockroach infested. After several unbearably hot days we decided to take in a movie just to relax and get out of the heat. The movie was *Rocky II*. It was about a fighter who fought his way out of poverty and became the heavyweight champ of the world. It was an inspiring story with a great theme song. Karen and I came out of the theater ready to take on the world.

The next day through a strange series of events, we found a trailer in the country owned by a professor at Anderson College. We closed the deal and headed back to Michigan for our belongings. We didn't own much in those days so we were able to move everything in our two cars and one pickup truck driven by a friend.

Once we had moved into our mobile home and had checked out the new area where we would be living, we had to make an important decision. It had to do with finances. Karen believed in budgeting our money but I wasn't in the habit of doing that. I agreed to try it. However, Karen needed to agree with me on tithing (giving 10% of our income back to God). We had received over $1000 in wedding money from friends and I felt we should tithe on it while Karen wasn't sure if we could afford to. It wasn't that Karen didn't tithe to the Lord, it was more a question of whether we needed to tithe on gifts. We decided to keep our account straight with God and believe that He would help our 90% stretch. He did.

The budgeting didn't work very well because it was hard to budget when we didn't know where the money would be coming from. It soon became apparent to both of us that we were on a faith adventure and only God knew how much we would need from week to week. As we were faithful to give Him our 10%, He was faithful to provide for us. Sometimes His provision came in the form of odd jobs such as yard work, phone sales, baby-sitting and tutoring. At other times, God provided by sending us unexpected money in the mail. God proved Himself faithful to us week after week. We lived under the blessing of God according to Malachi 3:8-12.

One of those odd jobs I decided to take was with the Army Reserves. Since I hoped to become an active duty military chaplain someday, I figured I might as well get started. I had heard that there was a position called chaplain candidate where I could serve as a chaplain in training. I called a recruiter and he told me I would need to be a part of a unit first before I could apply. Since I had a Bachelor's Degree in psychology I was eligible to work in the mental health field as a 91G, which was basically a medic that dealt with mental patients.

I was given the job and assigned to an Army reserve unit at Ft. Ben Harrison in Indianapolis. Much of my time was spent at the Veterans Hospital working with veterans who were classified as mental patients. For the next two years I served with professional people in that hospital setting. It turned out to be one of the best jobs I've ever had in the military.

However, I had been given some misinformation. It seemed I couldn't become a chaplain candidate while serving in another capacity in the Army. I would have to complete my two year obligation to my present unit first. Since Karen and I needed the money and I was having such a good time, I stayed in that unit and became an E-6 (Staff Sergeant) before I finally got out.

Once I was released from my Army obligation I tried to apply for a slot as chaplain candidate with the Army Reserves. However, I was told that I would have to wait until I graduated from seminary. I was depressed and prayed for wisdom to know what to do. It had all seemed so clear to me before I got out of my former unit that God was leading me every step

Getting In

of the way. Now I was confused. I couldn't figure out where I had missed God. My whole dream was to become a Chaplain, and now my goal was blocked.

In the meantime, the little United Methodist Church where we had worked with youth during our dating days urged me to consider becoming a member. I didn't know much about the denomination, so I was a bit hesitant. However, after studying the life of John Wesley and the history of the Methodist church, I decided to go for it. Almost immediately I was confronted by both the pastor and the members of that little church to pursue a vocation as a pastor or chaplain in the United Methodist denomination. It seemed like an impossibility at the time, but I began the procedure anyway. After an initial interview with the Board of Ordained Ministry, I was given temporary status.

However, the board was not very happy with my selection of Anderson School of Theology. They urged me to switch to a "recognized United Methodist Seminary." They felt that I was too conservative for the Methodist Church and therefore needed to be exposed to a more liberal theology which I would experience at any of the Methodist seminaries. I agreed to think about it. Before I left that conference room, I was handed a list of all the "recognized" seminaries.

About that time a friend of mine, Dart Liebrandt, who was a Second Lieutenant in the Indiana National Guard, told me about the chaplain candidate program in the National Guard. I made a few phone calls and discovered that I was eligible for the program. The application process involved a lot of paperwork. I had to have a complete physical, obtain an endorsement from my denominational headquarters in Nashville, and be fingerprinted by the local police to ensure that my record was clean.

Several months later on March 25, 1982, I was accepted and sworn in as a Chaplain Candidate, Second Lieutenant. I immediately applied for the next Chaplain Basic Training Course that ran from June 13 to July 23 of 1982. No one thought I had a chance of being accepted since I was so late in applying but I knew something that they didn't know. . . strange things happen when we ask God to help us. I was accepted. It was an exciting

 day when I reported for training at the Army Chaplain School located in FT. Monmouth, New Jersey. While in school I met Randy Heckert, who became one of my good friends. My goal was being fulfilled.

32

PASTOR DEN

When Karen and I were first married we decided that we didn't want to be in any leadership or ministry positions for the first year. We based this idea on Deuteronomy 24:5:

"If a man has recently married, he must not be sent to war or have any other duty laid on him. For one year he is to be free to stay at home and bring happiness to the wife he has married."

We didn't want to take that too literally but it seemed like a good general rule to follow as a newlywed couple. That first year we were very poor. A treat for us was to go to Wendy's and split a frosty and eat some of their free crackers. We lived in a trailer with walls that moved several inches when the wind blew. But we were happy. Karen was working on a Master's Degree at Ball State in deaf education and I was working on a Master's Degree in psychology and pastoral care at Anderson School of Theology. We both became graduate assistants which provided us with some much needed extra income.

In the spring, we received a phone call from a United Methodist District Superintendent (DS) asking if we would be interested in pastoring a church.

This same man had contacted us in the fall and we had declined because our first year as a married couple wasn't even close to being completed. We just didn't feel right about taking on a church in the fall, but when the spring rolled around and we were asked again, we were ready. In my devotions just that week I had been reading about the seven churches of Revelation (Rev 2-3). I was really impressed with the church of Philadelphia. I had no idea that the church I would be asked to take was Philadelphia United Methodist just outside Greenfield, Indiana.

We met the DS and he talked with us about the procedure of meeting for the first time with a group of people called the Pastor-Parish Relations Committee (PPR). When we arrived at the church the DS said to that committee, "Folks, this is your new pastor, Dennis Slattery, and his lovely wife, Karen." After a question and answer type interview, we were shown through the parsonage next door to the church and asked when we could start. We began in June of 1980.

One thing that surprised me was that the DS never came out to check up on me. I received no guidance from anyone but the members of that small church. They must have had this happen before because they took us under their wings and helped us along until we got the hang of things. We are still thankful to them for their patience, love and support.

My title was "Student Pastor" which meant that my job as a pastor was to be considered a part-time arrangement. My main responsibility was to be a student in seminary. Being a student pastor gave me an edge over the other students. They were always dealing with the theoretical aspects of what they were learning, while I dealt with how to apply the truths in a practical way in a ministry setting. The Methodist Church did a wonderful thing by providing up-coming pastors with such an opportunity. It gave us the opportunity to get on-the-job experience through our congregations.

One of the ideas that Karen and I tried in that church was discipleship. I had read a lot on the subject of discipleship and had tried to implement it whenever I could. The concept of discipleship is based on what Jesus did with His twelve apostles. He taught the masses but He also chose twelve to be with Him. Those few He trained and then sent them out. Then He supervised them while He was on the earth and gave them a ministry and a method to follow after He was gone. He shared inside information with the twelve that He didn't share with anyone else. Even the parables were

Pastor Den

only explained to the twelve so that anyone who wanted to know the interpretation would have to ask one of the twelve. In this way, He set them up to be in leadership.

With Jesus, class was always in session. The closest thing we have to discipleship in the modern world is an apprenticeship program that combines class work with on-the-job training. We use this concept to train doctors, nurses, dentists, plumbers, electricians, machinists, etc. It is also the method that Jesus used. If Jesus devoted three years of His life to discipling twelve men and they in turn, under the power of the Holy Spirit, went out and turned the world upside down, then His method was successful. Therefore, it is worth the effort to try and implement it today.

Karen and I began by meeting monthly for dinner with six couples (Marty & Onda Moran, Kevin & Sherry Miller, Mark & Linda Miller, Chris & Diane Miller, Gerry & Iris Shepherd, and Steve & Maureen Burns). After about six months I challenged the men individually to join me for Bible study. Most of them came. During our times together we studied the Bible, discussed Christian books, prayed, memorized Bible verses, and sang songs of praise. I also tried to involve the men in ministry by taking them to nursing homes to preach, hospitals to visit the sick, and homes in the community to witness. We had a great time together, holding each other accountable.

However, during those three years at the "Philly" Church Karen and I received frequent phone calls from Connie requesting that we take Glori for a while. The first year we took her for three months and the second year we took her for five months. We loved Glori and wanted her to live with us, but it was not to be. We grieved each time we had to give her back to Connie. It was during that time that Karen and I decided to start our own family.

33

KRISTIN

During the winter of 1981, Karen became pregnant. We were excited, but around Easter she miscarried and our hopes were dashed. It took several years for Karen to be healed from the trauma of that miscarriage, even though she became pregnant again almost immediately. As her second pregnancy continued it became apparent that there was something not quite right. She had high blood pressure and signs of protein in her urine. The diagnosis was toxemia.

About six weeks before delivery, Karen had to be hospitalized. When she started having other symptoms of advanced toxemia they decided on emergency surgery. I was not allowed in the operating room but I stood right by the operating room door so that I would be near. I hated being in the hallway away from the action. I wanted to be in that operating room with Karen so I knew what was going on, but in those days they wouldn't let dads in during "C" sections. After a long wait, word finally reached me that our new baby was a girl. I was standing in the hallway when the nurse brought her out all wrapped up. She looked so small and fragile and I was only allowed to gaze upon her for a few seconds before she was whisked away to a neo-natal ward.

I called Karen's parents right away and they decided to come as soon as they could get there. Since I had to wait for awhile to see Karen, I decided to make a few other calls to family and friends. After awhile I went down to the cafeteria for some breakfast. While I was eating two of the guys from our discipleship group showed up at the hospital to offer their support. Our daughter was born on a Sunday, so one of the guys volunteered to preach for me that day.

When I was finally able to see Karen, her first question was whether or not I had seen our new baby girl. When I told her I had we began to discuss names. We decided on Kristin Anne, born on April 4, 1982. However, when I told Karen we couldn't see Kristin yet because of some complications, I could see the disappointment in her eyes. Since Kristin was brought into the world several weeks early, and because of her pre-mature condition, she had to be in an incubator with tubes attached to her tiny body. Later that day they wheeled Karen's bed down to the nursery so she could see her new baby daughter. Kristin's condition was too fragile to allow her to be outside the incubator so Karen had to stick her hands through the small holes in the side.

That night we were told it was best for Kristin to go to the children's hospital several miles away. It was very difficult for Karen to watch her baby being packed up and taken away in an ambulance to another hospital, especially since she hadn't even held Kristin yet. But it seemed like that sacrifice would be best for our daughter, so we agreed to allow them to take her. When Karen's mom and dad arrived they were able to console her much better than I could. It was Karen's mom who was the first family member to actually hold Kristin.

Our discipleship group assisted and ministered to us through the whole ordeal. They came to the hospital to pray with us and offered their continued support and encouragement during those trying times. When Karen was released from the hospital she made daily trips to be with Kristin. Our baby was making good progress every day, even though her lungs were not fully developed. Ten days after her birth on April 14th (my birthday) Kristin came home. What a wonderful day that was. Kristin only weighed a little over five pounds when she came home from the hospital and she still seemed so thin and frail that we were hesitant to even give her a bath. Yet with Karen's mom right there we became more confident. Within a few days we worked out a routine and life went on.

One year later, as we were preparing to move to Michigan, Kristin took her first steps amid the boxes. How excited we were that day as she wobbled from mom to dad as we cheered her on. I was scheduled to graduate in May

Kristin

of 1983 with my second Master's Degree, a Master of Divinity. When that day arrived we loaded the moving van and with tears and prayers, left our student pastorate to head up to Michigan to become a full-time pastor.

34

DARCY

When I arrived at the Methodist parsonage in Ravenna, Michigan there was a man in the backyard working in what looked like a garden. I went out back and started a conversation with him and discovered that his name was Mike Wright. Mike was a radical Christian who decided to bless us by planting a garden behind the parsonage. Mike told me of his wife Glenna and his three children, but for the most part we talked about Jesus. It was exciting to meet someone who had such a strong love for the Lord.

Two days later my family and our furniture arrived. On that day we were blessed by another couple from our new church, Bill and Barb DeGroot, who came to mow the grass. After our first service in Ravenna, Bill and Barb invited us over for dinner. They were easy to get along with and had an obvious love for the Lord. Even Kristin, who was usually shy around strangers, went right up to "Mr. Bill." How great it was to meet enthusiastic Christians on our first days in a new ministry.

Karen and I started a discipleship group in the fall of that first year with about five couples. We had learned how important such a group is from our previous church. One of the highlights of those first few months was the trip I took with Mike Wright to Colorado Springs. We went to a Navigator conference on discipleship featuring Chuck Swindoll and Howard Hendricks. I wanted to expose Mike to the Navigators and other Christians who had a burden to win the world to Christ. We came home from that conference all fired up. As a result, we started several Navigator 2:7 small group Bible studies.

Christmas of that year was especially memorable. It was a joy to experience it with Kristin who was almost two years old and in awe of all the delights of the season. Karen surprised me with a very special card as we were opening our gifts on Christmas morning. Inside was a simple note written on the prescription pad of the local doctor. It simply read, "Congratulations, the test was positive." We were going to have another baby!

We carefully watched Karen's blood pressure during each month of her pregnancy, wondering if she would struggle with pre-eclamsia (toxemia) again. Everything seemed to be going fine during the first two trimesters so Karen attacked life with her typical 110% attitude. In her eighth month, the annual county fair took place. Our church traditionally ran a food stand. This was always a great time of fellowship and a terrific moneymaker. For some reason, this project looked as though it was not going to make it due to lack of a chairperson. Since Karen has a problem saying "No" to anyone, she volunteered to fill this gap. She coordinated donations, supplies and volunteers for the entire week of the Muskegon County fair. At the end of the week at her monthly check-up, her obstetrician put her on bed rest for the duration of the pregnancy. Though there is no solid evidence which proves that stress causes toxemia, she once again had all the symptoms after a stressful week at the fair.

Karen's mom came to help with the care of Kristin and to be sure Karen stayed put. Within a week, with doctor visits being her only outing, Karen's condition got worse. On Friday, August 10, 1984, I went with my wife to her appointment and we were sent across the street to Butterworth Hospital. A cancellation in the operating room made it possible for her to have a C-section immediately. This time I got to be with Karen every step of the way, and I was the first to hold our little 6-pound daughter. Though we had already decided on names, none of them seemed to fit this little bundle of joy. Somehow she just looked like "Darcy Joy."

Darcy was strong and healthy as compared to how her sister Kristin entered the world. She did, however, have ABO blood incompatibility, something we had never heard of before. This caused an elevated and prolonged jaundice type condition. An extra couple of days in the hospital

Darcy

and a few subsequent returns after her discharge to check her blood and to continue her biliribin treatments, and Darcy's "suntanned" complexion became pink and healthy.

We learned very early that Darcy had an exceptionally strong will, and knew how to express herself when she was not pleased with her feeding preferences or carrying positions. The people in our church were very excited about having a baby in the parsonage once again. Kristin now had someone to play with and our family seemed more complete. Our next-door neighbors had a son (Tony Way) born to them the day after Darcy was born. With that common denominator, we became friends and they eventually started attending our Church.

35

ORDINATION

In the fall of 1984, I applied for the final phase of ordination. I was required to preach a sermon on John 1 and write a paper stating my theology. It was a tedious task. I prayed about it constantly before actually submitting anything. Becoming an ordained elder in the Methodist church was required before I could pursue the chaplaincy. Therefore, I saw it as an important hurdle.

The interview for ordination was more than just a minor formality. As a Bible believing evangelical it was an uphill battle. I had been turned down once already because my beliefs seemed too radical for Methodists. I was told I needed to attend a more liberal seminary for one semester to be exposed to a wider range of ideas. It was there that I heard that God was a woman, the Bible wasn't true and that everyone including the devil would eventually be saved because God is all loving and would never hurt anyone. I opposed my instructors in public and in the required papers. Because of my "narrow views" on the authority of Scripture, I almost failed my courses. Instead of becoming liberal, I became more radical for Christ. Later I would discover that all evangelical, Bible believing candidates for ordained ministry were put through some of the same kinds of harassment that I went through.

I filled out the paperwork and did all of the assigned tasks for my ordination packet. I then sent it in to the Board of Ordained Ministry. About a month later I was informed that I would be interviewed at Wesley Woods in March of 1985. If I passed that interview I would be ordained in June by the Bishop at Annual Conference.

MARCH 1985

I turned away from the window and began pacing back and forth in the lobby of the Wesley Woods lodge awaiting the answer of the interviewing committee. The committee had asked some tough questions and I wasn't sure if they liked my answers. In many ways I was too conservative to be a Methodist. They weren't sure about my views on salvation and baptism. I didn't believe in universalism (everyone including the devil is saved in the end). I believed people were born into this world as sinners who are out of fellowship with God. For them to be saved they need to repent of their sins and trust in Christ for their salvation. Those ideas are very similar to what John Wesley preached but sound strange to many modern Methodists. On baptism, I held that people are not converted by being baptized. Baptism is an outward sign of an inner reality. My ideas were very close to those of the Evangelical Brethren who merged with the Methodists in 1968.

One of the questions that stumped me was, "What do you do for fun?" I didn't have any hobbies. For the Army I lifted weights, ran several miles, and did correspondence courses. With my family I went for walks, camped in a tent, and just spent time together. If I wanted to relax I'd sit down and read a book. I struggled to answer that question and wondered if my floundering would disqualify me for the ministry. Could I be disqualified for not having a hobby?

I started pacing back and forth again, praying that God would grant me favor with the people who were deciding my future. As I paced back and forth, I kept retracing the steps that had finally brought me to this place in life. It had been a long journey, one I never thought I would take: from a tough Marine atheist in Vietnam to a radical Bible believing pastor. Even my own mother found it hard to believe. What a mighty God we serve!

"Dennis Slattery?" It was one of the men from the committee that had just interviewed me.

Ordination

"Yes, right here," I responded.
"The committee is ready to see you now. Follow me."

My hands were sweating and my stomach was tied in a knot as I walked back into that small room. I sat back in the "hot seat" to await the verdict.

"This committee has decided to recommend you for full membership as an ordained elder in the West Michigan Conference. Congratulations."

I drove home praising God. What an amazing thing God had done in my life.

To prepare for the ordination service I had to select one layperson and one clergyperson to accompany me in the processional. For the layperson I chose John Beukers. John was from the little church where Karen and I had once worked with youth. John and his beautiful wife Joan were instrumental in my becoming a Methodist pastor. The clergyperson I chose was Dave Flagel who pastored a nearby church and had become a friend that I trusted. I also needed a banner for the occasion. My banner was made by a gifted artist in the Ravenna Church, Shirley Smith. The banner had the words on it, ***"Go Make Disciples."*** I felt those words taken from Matthew 28:19 very aptly described my mission in life from the Lord.

On June 15, 1985, I marched in the ordination processional held in the chapel on the campus of Albion College. That day a group of people laid their hands on me and ordained me to full-time Christian service. I was told to take authority and to preach The Word. It was an exhilarating moment.

The next day I filled out the paper work to become an Army Chaplain for the National Guard. It took nine months to become a reality. I had jumped through one more hoop. Now I was just that much closer to reaching my ultimate goal of becoming an active duty chaplain.

36

DAD

Being a dad is one of the toughest roles in life. I was never given a manual on fathering, even though I needed one desperately. Like most men I wanted to be about the task of conquering my world while I was still young enough to do it. At the end of the day my energy was usually spent and I felt like coming home to relax. The last thing I felt like doing was engaging my wife in a deep conversation or playing with the kids. That doesn't mean that I didn't love them, it just meant I was tired. Yet those first eighteen years of their lives go by so quickly. How ironic that they coincide with the same years most men are out trying to find success. While I love kids, I admit that I have struggled with trying to be a good father. I certainly don't have it all together in that area.

I failed terribly at that task with Kescia and Glori. It is hard to be a good father when you are separated by 1500 miles from your children. I have tried to stay in touch with them over the years through letters, calls and visits. Once or twice a year we either go to Florida or try to bring them up to Michigan. But it has been tough. Paying weekly child support, sending gifts, and those occasional visits never seem to be enough. When anything bad ever happened in their lives, I somehow ended up being blamed for it. Their mom has had a tough life and yet has tried to provide for the girls by often working several odd jobs just to make ends meet. While we haven't always agreed on how the girls should be raised, I do give her a lot of credit for sticking in there with them through a lot of hard times. However, most of their values and perspectives on life have come from their mother and not from me. Therefore, they tend to see the world the same way that their mother does. In comparison, my influence in their lives has been very small.

However, with my other children, I have had more of an impact because we see each other every day. We talk, pray, eat, and play together. I have tried to teach them the lessons that I have learned from life. Those lessons are based on my successes and failures. A day rarely passes without us expressing love for each other through hugs, kisses, and even saying the words, "I love you." I have also taught them about the Lord and the hope that He gives us. I have shared with them the changes that God did in my life through Jesus Christ. Karen has had an even greater impact on their lives than I have. She has devotions with them every day out of the Bible and teaches them to memorize Bible verses through songs and games. She reads them stories about famous Christians making it so interesting that they often rush off to tell their friends. By the grace of God, all of our children have invited Christ into their lives and are trying to live a life pleasing to God. My prayer is that they would not repeat the same mistakes that I have made. Many of my mistakes were the same mistakes that my father made. Could that be what God meant when He said that the sins of the fathers would be carried on to the third and fourth generations (Exodus 20:5)?

Let me tell you about my family. I was born on Good Friday, April 14, 1949 in Muskegon, Michigan. I was the middle of three children and the only boy. My older sister was named after our grandmother, Helen, but she usually went by her middle name, Patricia (Pat). My younger sister was Vickie. Each of us are about a year and a half apart. At about the age of two my parents moved to Jackson, Michigan where I spent the majority of my growing up years. My dad was a salesman with *Swift & Company* but he also worked several part-time jobs at night. Since he was gone a lot of the time, I didn't really know him very well. My mom tried to make up for that by spending most of her time with us. On week-ends we usually went to Church as a family, then out to eat and later to a movie. My mom was a good woman who felt it was her duty to train us in how to behave in public places like restaurants, theaters, library's and parties. From my earliest recollection, I remember going with my parents to square dances. As I grew older I developed an interest in dancing and learned how to do the cha-cha, polka, twist, monkey, the funky chicken, and any other dance that was popular at the time. I have always had a good sense of rhythm and at one time even played the bongos as part of a church orchestra.

My dad and I didn't get along very well during the formative years of my life. He was too busy trying to conquer his world to be a good father. Not that he didn't try, he just didn't know what to do in the days before *Focus on the Family* and all the "how to" parent manuals available today. I always had a lot of energy and just seemed to find trouble without having to look very hard. I think my dad was probably tired and frustrated from working so many hours that he needed to find an outlet for his pent up anger, so at times, when it became too much, he took it out on his kids. From my perspective, rarely did a day pass when I didn't get spanked as a child. Many of those spankings I probably deserved, but I rarely saw the balance of love to go along with it. However, the verbal abuse in the long run had a greater effect on my life than anything else. The words that he said to me or about me have lived to haunt me.

"You're so stupid, you can't do anything right. Why can't you be more like your sister Pat? You always do what anyone suggests. Would you jump off a cliff if someone dared you to? You're gonna end up in a home for juvenile delinquents or on the street like a bum. Is that what you want?"

According to my dad, I was the black sheep of the family that ruined everything for everyone else. I was a failure. During those dark years of my life, I determined that I didn't want to be anything like my dad. When I became a teenager the conflict intensified. He threatened me continually, often saying he was going to personally put me in a juvenile home. I often dreamed of the day when I would be bigger than him. Eventually, my bitterness grew into hatred. Nothing I did ever seemed good enough for him, so I gave up trying.

When I turned seventeen my dad ran off with another woman and divorced my mom. The day he left I rejoiced. I was glad he was gone. My sisters and I pitched in and helped my mom during those trying months right after the split. We didn't see dad for several years.

Just before I left for basic training with the Marines, my mom begged him to come and talk to me about the realities of war. He had served on a destroyer in the Pacific with the Navy during WWII, so she felt he knew something of what it would be like for me. Yet at that time he was the last person I wanted to talk to about anything. I didn't respect his opinion, so his visit seemed like a waste of time.

However, during my stay in Vietnam, he and his new wife wrote to me. Those letters helped bring about some healing in our relationship. By the time my tour was over, we got together and were able to push the past aside somewhat and act civilized with each other. However, pushing the past aside was not the same as being healed of painful memories. I still had a lot of anger deep within that I didn't know how to deal with, so I just suppressed it. I now know that the way to find healing is to shed light on all the dark areas of our past. When I invited Jesus Christ, The Light of the world, into my life, His light eventually revealed all those dark areas.

One of the verses in the Bible that really bothered me said that I had to forgive everyone if I expected God to forgive me (Matt. 6:14-15). The first person I thought of was Connie. It took me several years to reach a point where I could forgive her. Yet even as I was dealing with trying to forgive Connie, the Lord reminded me of another relationship that needed healing - - my dad. To forgive is an act of mercy that comes from the will. It's a decision that we make mentally and then need to express verbally. The feelings will eventually line up with our decision and continual confession. When I discovered that truth I began confessing with my mouth, "I forgive my dad. . . I forgive my dad." This helped some, as did the many prayers I sent up to the Lord asking Him to make it a reality. However, God's way of making it a reality was not exactly the same as my idea. Doing it God's way meant I had to confront my dad in person and speak those words of forgiveness right to his face.

"OK, Lord, if You want me to do this, You're going to have to help me find him because I don't even know where he is."

Right about that time my church decided to provide me with some training in *Evangelism Explosion*, a visitation style of evangelism started by

Dad

Dr. D. James Kennedy. My training would be at the place where it all began, Coral Ridge Presbyterian Church in Ft. Lauderdale, Florida. Coral Ridge was a church that Dr. Kennedy built up from 17 people to about 10,000 using the principles of Evangelism Explosion. Karen and I had some good friends, Bob & Sherry Chalice, living near Dr. Kennedy's church. They were gracious enough to invite our whole family to stay with them during my training.

One night Karen and I were driving north on Route 1 and I remembered that my grandparents, Guy and Helen Slattery, had lived just off that road in Pompano Beach. I had only been to their house a few times before they died but as I drove through the area I recognized several landmarks. When I found the right road I pulled in and drove up to the house. I was apprehensive as I walked to the door, rang the doorbell and waited. A woman opened the door and I explained who I was and that my grandparents had once lived in this house. She told me that she leased it from a man named Ken. Ken was an old friend of the family. I found his phone number and made arrangements to get together. Through our visit with Ken and his wife Millie, I was able to get a lead on my dad. It took a while to make contact but eventually we did.

After dinner one evening, Dad wanted to show us around Fort Lauderdale. It was during that tour that I confronted him with the past. Things became very quiet in the car as I unfolded some of the hurt that had been inflicted on me as a child.

"Dad, for all the pain you caused me both physically and mentally, I forgive you. And if I have caused you pain, I ask that you forgive me."

My dad continued to drive keeping his eyes on the road ahead. He didn't say much about it but our relationship hasn't been the same since. In some ways it's like we've started over with a clean slate. We can now talk honestly and freely. Forgiving each other changed our relationship.

As a pastor I have worked with many people who are struggling in this very area. The hurts are often so deep that they seem beyond repair. I know that forgiving someone or seeking someone's forgiveness is a very difficult thing to do for most people. Emotional pain runs deep and is hard to let go of. Pride hinders us from going to others, as if our seeking them out is an admission of our own weakness or blame in the matter. But there is freedom that comes when we give forgiveness to others and receive forgiveness for our own mistakes. God is a merciful God and He wants us to be merciful too. We don't forgive others because they deserve it. If all of us got what we deserve we would all be burning in Hell this very moment. We forgive because the Lord commands us to forgive (Mark 11:25-26). And we forgive because we have been forgiven (Matt 18:21-35).

Jesus taught me that life is too short to carry a grudge. As we move through life we can't help but get our feelings hurt by someone. God has given all of us the freedom to choose to do good things that help people or bad things that can hurt them. But if we carry a grudge and harbor bitterness in our heart regarding that person who treated us wrongly, then those feelings develop the power, over time, to destroy us. Maybe that's why Jesus taught us to regularly offer forgiveness to those who hurt us. Even in the Lord's Prayer we deal with this issue;

"Forgive us our sins, as we forgive those who sin against us."
(Matt 6:12)

In essence, we are asking God not to forgive us unless we forgive others. By an act of my will I forgave my dad, Connie, and a whole group of other people who did bad things to me. I gave up my hatred for those people by giving it to Jesus. Somehow He replaced it with a love that I can't comprehend or produce. I guess that's how the Lord backs up our obedience to His Word. He performs the miracle after we obey. At least He did for me.

Wherever you are, Dad, in spite of everything, God loves you and so do I.

37

D.J.

When 1986 began, I wrote down in my journal 10 goals for the New Year. One of those goals was to have another baby. Yes, I have been accused of being very methodical before, perhaps that's why I'm a Methodist. John Wesley and his followers were first called Methodists because they were so regimented in their service of God - - 4:00 AM Pray; 5:00 AM Preach; 6:00 AM Study; etc. I tend to be much the same.

In April, I noted in my diary that I thought Karen might be pregnant because she was acting very emotional and seemed to tire easily. Over the years I have learned to tell when Karen is pregnant by just watching her. On May 1st our suspicions were confirmed - - the doctor told us Karen was due in December.

The more we thought about having a baby in December the stranger it seemed. It was so inconvenient for the rest of the family, just thinking of what an imposition a baby would be. How could we make plans for family get togethers, parties, Church plays, and all the rest? Our plans were being interrupted at the busiest time of year. And like most parents we wondered, what baby can possibly have decent birthday parties when overshadowed by Christmas? The only advantage seemed to be a tax break at the end of the year. But Karen was pregnant and we both love kids, so there was no turning back.

As Karen grew in size we went through all the normal preparations for having a baby:

-Will it be a boy or girl?
-What should we name this child?
-What room would the baby occupy?
-What do we need to do to the house to prepare?
-Which Doctor do we go to?

As a pastor I tend to view things a bit different from many people. Knowing our baby would be born in December, I often wondered during the pregnancy about Joseph & Mary - - what preparations did they make for their baby? Did they prepare a house? Did they ever see a doctor? They knew it would be a boy and they knew they were to call Him Jesus. But they were still human and it was their first child - - surely they must have had some concerns like any normal couple.

Karen had already gone through two C-sections, so we assumed this next child would also be born into the world via C-section. Her due date was slotted for December 26, so the doctor felt fairly certain that scheduling her surgery for December 19 should work out fine.

By Thanksgiving Karen was showing signs of toxemia (high blood pressure, protein in the urine, and swelling). We had been through this with both Kristin and Darcy. I wondered if Mary had any complications or problems?

We began to meet with our doctor every five days. By then he had some questions about the exact date to do the C-section. I couldn't help but wonder if Joseph and Mary ever wondered about the exact due date. But then I was reminded of the verse that says, *"At just the right time Jesus came"* (Gal 4:4, my own version)

I was reassured that at just the right time our child would also be born. On Friday December 12 we saw the doctor and he told us to come in on Monday for a non-stress test. Sunday was a very busy day with Church, Sunday School, a progressive dinner, and an evening fellowship reunion meeting. We didn't get home till after 9:00. We put the kids to bed and then put our selves to bed. At 3:15 in the morning Karen woke me up and told me to get out of bed. Her water had broken and she was having regular contractions. I called the doctor and he advised us to get to the hospital right away. I asked our next door neighbor, Sue Way, to watch our kids as we headed for the hospital. As I drove from Ravenna to Grand Rapids at 65-75 MPH (in a 55 MPH zone) on a foggy night, I tried to give Karen instructions on breathing. Since we had problems with the birth of our two previous girls, causing them to come into the world earlier than anticipated, we had never dealt with contractions and special breathing instructions that accompany normal deliveries. So this was a first for us. In the midst of it all, in the back of my mind, I wondered when Mary's water broke? Did it happen while she was riding the donkey? Did they have to rush to Bethlehem? Did Joseph act like most husbands? Did Mary know how to breathe? Did Joseph help her?

When we arrived at the hospital, I pulled up to the emergency room entrance where we were met by a security guard with parking instructions and a nurse with a wheel chair. As I went off to park the car, I thought about the reception that Joseph and Mary received, "No Room!" There were no nurses, doctors, or security guards. They couldn't even find a room to get out of the cold night air. The only comfort they got was in a barn surrounded by animals.

After signing Karen in as a patient and filling out insurance forms, I was allowed to go find my wife. She was in a labor room with a nurse nearby monitoring the baby's heart, as well as keeping a close eye on the contractions. One hour later we were in the operating room. As I glanced around I couldn't help but notice how clean and sterile everything was. The floors were shinning, the walls and ceiling seemed to sparkle, and all the people in the room had on hats, masks, special robes, gloves, and booties. Sitting on a stool beside my wife, I tried to picture what it must have been like to deliver a baby in a barn, where nothing was sterile or even clean. Baby Jesus was born in such a setting.

Karen's C-section went great. When the head popped out the doctor said, "Well no eyebrows, it's probably a girl. Most of the babies I deliver without eyebrows turn out to be girls."

Just then the rest of the body came out, "It's a boy!"

I looked at Karen and repeated the words, "Karen, it's a boy!"

As they took our new son across the room to clean him off, I wondered if Joseph and Mary were excited when Jesus finally appeared. Did Joseph say to Mary, "It's a boy!"

I think all parents want to have a child their own gender. While I loved my girls with all my heart, I was ecstatic to have a son. I had prayed God would one day give me a son and now I saw God's faithfulness to answer that prayer. I couldn't wait to tell someone. I called Karen's parents first. They cried tears of joy over the phone. Karen's dad was the only one in the family who had predicted our next child would be a boy and he was right. (It should be noted that he has never been wrong on guessing the gender of his grandkids). Next I called Sue Way who was watching our girls. As I made other phone calls I thought about the angels who were so excited about the birth of Jesus that they went and told the shepherds nearby that a Savior had been born in Bethlehem.

Later, as I drove home, the song *Joy To The World* came on the radio. As I looked up toward heaven, I shouted "Joy to the world, I have a son!" But then I thought about the meaning of the song - - *Joy to the world the Lord has come. Let earth receive her King, Let every heart prepare Him room.* My son was not a king, nor was he the Lord of Glory. Yet his birth brought great joy to my heart. However, when compared to the birth of Jesus, my son's birth was not very significant to the rest of the world. For no one greater than Jesus has ever been born into this world. Everyone should be joyful over the birth of Jesus Christ because His birth has changed our world forever. Each year people make a big deal about Christmas but they often fail to recognize it as the birthday of the Lord Jesus. The prophet Isaiah predicted,

"Unto us a child is born, unto us a Son is given: and the government shall be upon His shoulder; and His name shall be called Wonderful, Counselor, The Mighty God, The Everlasting Father, The Prince of Peace." (Isaiah 9:6)

I praise God for the birth of Jesus and the birth of our son, whom we named Derek James (D.J.). Both events drastically affected my life!

38

TWO CHURCHES AT ONCE

There are several things that I love about the pastorate - - preaching, teaching, evangelism, and discipleship. I have often been told that those are areas of giftedness for me. I even enjoy doing weddings and funerals because I find that they are great opportunities for ministry. I also love to help people who know they need Jesus. My friend Rose Sims always says that Jesus and the eternal life that He offers will one day be everyone's greatest need. I agree with Rose and love to share Christ with people. Yet people also need help with meeting everyday needs like food, clothes, paying bills, and even counseling during crisis situations in their lives. Most pastors I know went into the ministry to help people with just those kinds of problems.

But being a pastor can be very difficult as well. I have learned from experience that it is impossible to please everyone in any given congregation because we all view life differently. There are always three ways to do anything: the right way, the wrong way and the perfect way. Unfortunately, not everyone will agree on that which is perfect. Therefore, leading any group of people will eventually result in criticism over something. I have been criticized for my choice in clothes, ties, shoes, socks and cars. Some people have not liked my beard, mustache, or side burns. Others have made negative comments on the way I comb my hair, the way I tie my ties, and the way I shine my shoes. Some parishioners have not liked the way I do announcements, prayer requests, bulletins, newsletters, and hymn selection. In one Church, I was told that asking people to shake hands at the beginning of the service was "turning the Church into a bar room." People have made comments on how I open letters, whom to visit or not visit, how to preach, how to counsel people, and even how to decorate our own personal Christmas tree. One lady actually came into our house and started redecorating our Christmas tree, without being asked to do so. Needless to say we were offended. (Are pastor's allowed to get offended?)

Not everyone is so negative. If they were there probably wouldn't be anyone who would want to be a pastor and undergo such abuse. Many people are kind and sweet in their interactions with other believers, including their pastors. Fortunately, I have received more compliments than complaints, it's just that the complaints seem to stand out. I believe that all people tend to focus on the negative and find it easier to point out someone's faults than their good points. And we all have faults, including pastors, but we also have feelings that get hurt when people rudely step on us and the things we hold dear. In every church that we have served in we have people that we stay in contact with and consider them to be dear friends. As a matter of fact, I have people from every Church we have worked in who still pray for me and my ministry. I thank God for those dear saints and consider it a privilege to be counted as their friends.

When I was in seminary, we were taught that if we were "there" for our people during the tough moments in their lives that they would love us forever. However, I have discovered, through real life situations, that it isn't always true. People can very easily turn on a pastor. We often become a convenient scapegoat for the congregations we serve. People don't seem to realize that we are human beings who are subject to pain just like anyone else. According to some studies, hardly a day goes by in America without some pastor quitting the ministry. Why? By far the main reason would be discouragement due to criticism by the people they are called to serve. People can be vicious and do it all in the name of the Lord. I think the devil is often involved in this critical attack to keep the church from accomplishing anything significant for the Lord.

Serving one church had proven to be very challenging. Therefore, I was a little skeptical when my DS told me that my next assignment would involve pastoring two churches at once. Climax and Scotts United Methodist Churches had just experienced a split brought on by their former pastor. I was told that he didn't like the Methodist system, so he left the denomination and took 120 people with him to start a new church in the same community. Families were split and people felt betrayed. My wife and I were being sent in to try to bring about a healing.

We met with the Board of the new churches in January and moved into the parsonage on April 1 (no fooling). Karen had just delivered our newest member of the family on December 15, 1986. We now had three children: Kristin 4, Darcy 2, and D.J. who was an infant.

About ten days before we moved, I received a call from the Pentagon. I had mentioned to the National Guard chaplain at the Pentagon that I was looking for a slot on active duty. He called to say he had a slot. My heart skipped a beat. This was my dream of a lifetime, to be an active duty chaplain.

Yet I heard myself saying a strange thing, "I can't do it."

"Why not?" he asked.

"Because I've made a commitment to a new Church. I have to start on the first of April. I can't back out. Those people are hurting and they're counting on me."

My friend didn't understand but I was sure God did. I committed it to the Lord in prayer.

"Lord, if you want me on active duty as a chaplain you're going to have to work out the details of when and how. I believe you have led us to this new church and I have made a commitment to those people. My life and my future are in your hands, Lord."

My first Sunday at Climax was a memorable one. I usually get up early and go to church to preach through my sermon for the angels and Jesus. If they like it I preach it as it is, if not I make changes. That first Sunday in April 1987, I went to church early to work prayerfully on my sermon and then returned home. After a while we received a phone call.

"Pastor, are you coming to Church today?"

"Sure I am. I'll be there on time."

"OK, we'll just sing some songs till you get here."

"What do you mean?" I asked.

"Didn't you set your clock ahead last night?" Michigan had just switched to Daylight Savings Time. We didn't realize it because of our move. We had been too busy to watch TV or listen to the radio and we hadn't seen a paper in days.

Embarrassed I rushed to the church and sure enough, they were singing a few songs. They laughed with me over my mistake and never let me forget that day. Yet those wonderful people took us in and gave us more love than we ever gave to them.

During my time at those churches, I was assigned to a different Army National Guard unit. Previously, I had been assigned to the 3rd battalion of the 126 Infantry. However, because of my change of location, due to a new church appointment, I was reassigned to a tank unit, the 246 Armor out of Dowagiac. My main contact person for coordination with that unit was Captain Jim Wilson. Jim and I became friends and developed a good working relationship together. The former chaplain of the unit was also a friend of mine, Mike Brallier. Mike had taken a new church in Muskegon, so we simply switched National Guard units. Being an old infantryman at heart, I wasn't sure if I was going to like being in a tank unit, but those tankers of the 246 didn't hold that against me. They just took me as I was and taught me how to minister to men that eat a lot of dust and are really into "heavy metal." In both the Army and the church I was enjoying my new assignment. Life was great!

39

JESUS WANTS YOU

One day I was sitting at my desk going over a pile of mail that contained many training events for pastors. As I looked at the opportunities I prayed, "God, there are a lot of great opportunities here that I could take advantage of, but I need to know which one You want me to go to. Help me to know Your will."

In an attitude of prayer I grabbed each brochure and held it up to the Lord asking, "This one?" The answer I kept getting was "NO!" Until I finally hit upon the right one and God gave me a "YES!" I looked at the advertisement. It was for the Holy Spirit and World Evangelization Conference in New Orleans. It was scheduled for the hottest time of the summer. I wasn't sure this was God. I knew my wife wouldn't like the idea either. "God are you sure? Wouldn't it be better if I went to this conference on church growth in nearby Chicago?" Silence. I looked at the mailing again. "Lord if this is from you I need YOU to work out all the details including convincing my wife and providing for me to go."

I didn't say anything to anyone for a few days. I have discovered that whenever I tell people God is leading me to do this or that I usually receive criticism. Not everyone who claims to be a Christian has a desire to seek or receive guidance from God. When I did reveal it to my wife she said it didn't make any sense to go to New Orleans and that we couldn't afford it. I agreed but said we would have to wait and see what God had in store. Each time I prayed about it God gave me the silent treatment. I told God that I had to know if this was His will. I needed a sign. If I knew this was His will then I would just move out and do it, but I needed to know for sure.

About that time I attended a Good News Conference on the campus of Taylor University in Northern Indiana. During a lunch break I wandered through the library. I have a real love for books and enjoy just browsing around. I went upstairs and walked into the magazine section. There were hundreds of magazines on display. I walked up and down the aisles looking at all the different kinds of magazines without picking up any. As I came to the very end of the final magazine rack, one magazine caught my eye so I reached over and picked it up. As I opened it, there was a huge advertisement on the first page I looked at. As I read the words I was stunned, for I saw in those words a message from God to me. Printed in bold large letters was this message:

"JESUS WANTS YOU IN NEW ORLEANS"

I closed the magazine and said to the Lord, "God that's good enough for me. I'm going!"

Once I committed myself to going to New Orleans all the details concerning the trip came together. When I arrived at the conference one of the seminars I felt guided to by God was led by one of the men in leadership at Elim Bible Institute where I had attended. This particular man was the main person who influenced me to quit college and marry Connie. I had forgiven him several times in my own private prayer life, thinking that was all that was needed. I was wrong. God impressed upon me the need to go to him and personally forgive him just like I did with my dad. I knew that many of the speakers at these events didn't show up until the last minute and then were surrounded by people after the message, so I asked the Lord to make it possible for me to talk to him privately. When I arrived at the conference room he was already there. I went up to him explaining who I was. Then I pulled him aside and reviewed my story and his part in my decision to leave school and get married without any courtship. I told him about the pain that decision had caused. Finally, I told him what I felt God had wanted me to say to him, "For your part in this, I forgive you!"

The rest of the conference was great. Along with about 50,000 other people, I praised the Lord in song and dance. It didn't seem like I learned any new deep truth during those few days in New Orleans but I was obedient to God. I did what God wanted me to do and that was the lesson I took home with me.

When I arrived back in Michigan miracles began to happen. I didn't feel any different but God just began to use me in new ways. It seemed to me that God was blessing my ministry because of my obedience. Yet other new lessons were just around the corner.

40

IT NEVER HURTS TO ASK

    One day I was asked to visit a 40 year old woman who was dying. She had two small children still at home to care for. She was in an Intensive Care Unit in a Kalamazoo hospital. My first visit with her was very short. Her kidneys had failed and her liver had shut down. The doctors gave her at best 48 hours to live. Her eyes looked like they were going to come right out of their sockets, and tubes were everywhere. I quickly introduced myself and said I wanted to pray for her. I prayed for her healing, rebuked death, and left. The next day I did the same.
    I have come to understand that death can be invited or rebuked. In the Bible it speaks of the angel of death, as in the story of the Israelites in Egypt (Exodus 9-12). Jude 9 speaks of Michael the archangel fighting with the devil for the dead body of Moses. Many people during their final moments of life on earth often speak of angels in the room sent to escort them from one realm to the other. Therefore, if I go in to see someone who is near death, depending on the situation, I will often rebuke the angel/spirit of death before I offer a prayer for healing.
    On the third visit, as I took her hand and started praying, I saw in my mind some internal organ that looked black and diseased. I prayed for God to heal that organ, and in my mind I saw it turning pink. I rebuked the spirit of death and asked for a total healing. I prayed for tissues and organs to function properly and for her to be able to get out of that hospital. To the

amazement of everyone, she was completely healed. When she was strong enough I invited her to my church to share what the Lord had done. After the service she said something I will never forget.

"I had a lot of people visit me in the hospital. Many of them even prayed with me. But no one prayed for me to be healed but you. Thanks."

This story illustrates a wonderful truth about prayer: IT NEVER HURTS TO ASK. I don't understand everything about healing but I do know that God has given us hundreds of promises in the Bible which indicate that He will answer our prayers. Why did He do that? Is it to tease us by giving us false hope? No. He gave us all those promises to encourage us to ask for His help. I have found that many times God's failure to get involved in our situation is simply because we haven't asked. People often say that God helps those who help themselves but that couldn't be further from the truth. The Bible says that God helps those who ask for His help. In James 4:2 we are reminded that we don't have because we don't ask.

Prayer is a real mystery. It is touching the unseen. It is the force that moves the hand of God. John Wesley, the founder of the Methodist church, once said, "God does nothing but in answer to prayer." I believe he meant that God has limited Himself by allowing us the privilege to pray. If we pray He gets involved and if we don't, He stands back. God is still sovereign and can do whatever He wants with or without us. Yet, the point is that He wants to involve us in the process.

Based on my observations, I believe there are times when we refuse to pray over situations in our life because we think God doesn't want to be bothered by our insignificant concerns when He has major world problems to contend with. Yet I believe that God wants us to pray about everything (Philippians 4:6-7). If it concerns us, because He is our heavenly Father, it concerns Him too. Therefore, we shouldn't be afraid to ask. We may not control the results, but we can sure hinder God's involvement if we fail to bring our concerns to His attention. Whether it is a prayer to stop mosquitoes from biting us or a prayer for the healing of a friend, "It never hurts to ask!"

41

SETTING THE CAPTIVE FREE

Believing that God can answer prayer is one thing, but believing He will do it NOW to help people be set free is another deal altogether. Yet as a pastor, my job is helping people. However, the problems that some people have today are so severe that many pastors don't want to even attempt to help them. Therefore, many referrals are made to mental health facilities. A problem with this is that most mental health facilities counsel from a purely secular point of view, void of any belief in God. I realize that some people need an in-house program to protect both society and themselves. Yet, the Church needs to rethink the whole issue of referrals to secular mental health facilities and to reconsider what Christians might be able to offer those seeking help.

On dealing with people's problems, psychology has given us some very valuable insights. I personally enjoy this field of study which is why I spent the time to earn both a Bachelor's Degree and Master's Degree in psychology.

But psychology hasn't gone far enough. From my own experience and a lengthy search of the Bible, I have discovered that some problems just can't be solved simply by psychology alone. We need a Biblical understanding of people. People are created in the image of God. We have a mind, body and SPIRIT, unlike the animal kingdom. I really appreciate the efforts of Dr. James Dobson, Dr. Larry Crabb and the doctors associated with the

Minirth-Meier Clinic for their emphasis on the Bible. All of those men are committed Christians and professionals in the mental health field. They try to offer the best insights from both psychology and the Bible. Yet those men are the exceptions. The majority of psychologists approach their profession from a much more secular point of view.

Therefore, the real conflict with psychology comes when we begin to discuss sin and spirituality as described in the Bible. God has given us a free will to choose right from wrong. What God considers wrong behavior is called sin; failing to measure up to God's standard of perfection. The reason there is so much crime, violence, suffering and war in this world is because people have been given the freedom to choose how they will behave. God doesn't usually step in to stop the bullet of a murderer nor does he intercept the attack of every rapist. There are exceptions, but for the most part God doesn't intervene. He allows people the freedom of choice even when they make bad choices which hurt other people.

However, while freedom of choice and sin explain some things, there are often questions as to why some people do such grotesque things, such as killing their family members, mutilating bodies, having sex with babies, mass killings, etc. Even suicide often seems bizarre and unexplainable. In addition, cruelty to animals, cannibalism, decapitation and human sacrifices to Satan are also common crimes in America today. But why? How can people do such things? This type of human behavior seems to be in a different category from all the rest. It is not easily explained by psychologists except to simply categorize it as abnormal behavior.

The Bible, however, offers some interesting insight into this area of human behavior. The Bible indicates that people are influenced by a spirit world which is invisible to us. In this spirit world there are good forces and evil forces. The good forces are the holy angels of God who try to help people and encourage them to live a holy life for God. On the opposing side are evil spirits (demons) trying to harm people and get them to sin. These two forces are constantly fighting. Yet it is a war we usually can't see.

As I was studying for my Bachelor's Degree in psychology in the late 1970's, I was told that evil forces don't really affect human behavior unless we are superstitious enough to believe that nonsense. When I went on to study for a Master's Degree in psychology and pastoral care, I discovered that most people in the mental health field dismiss all of Jesus' dealings with evil spirits by saying that He was just accommodating Himself to the superstitions of His day and age. I couldn't understand why Jesus would do that when He was very vocal about correcting other wrong ideas. Therefore, I had trouble with that conclusion and decided to do my Master's thesis on the topic of demon possession. I explored the Biblical understanding and found that we use a non-Biblical term to describe the condition. The word for demon possession is never used but another Greek word is found repeatedly. The Greek word is "diamonizomai" which is translated in the King James version as "demon possessed" but is more properly rendered "demonized." To be "demonized" is to come under the influence of a demon, while the term "possessed" carries with it the idea of total ownership. People are never owned by demons but they can be influenced by them.

Historically, people from every part of our globe have believed that there is another realm where spirits exist. Even though modern psychologists of the western world have tried to rid us of these "primitive superstitious beliefs", it is evident to many people that our world is still being influenced by some unseen force. While science-fiction buffs believe we are under the watchful eye of aliens from another planet, the Bible describes it in terms of a spirit realm with good and bad forces. Suffice it to say that there is something out there whose presence can occasionally be felt even by atheistic psychologists with such intensity that it will cause the hair on the back of their necks to stand up.

I am certain this is real. I have both seen them and fought with them. This is no joke. We are in a battle with evil forces that we can't detect with the naked eye, and more often than not, people are defeated because they don't understand this enemy.

Such was the case with a young woman named Jane who came to me for counseling. Jane had been under a psychiatrist's care for over two years. She had been diagnosed with Multiple Personality Disorder (MPD). She had the ability to become nine different people. Her voice could change to sound like a man even though she was a petite mother of two small children. At times she was suicidal. At other times she exhibited enthusiasm about life. She would often roll into a ball on the floor and become totally dysfunctional, yet at still other times she seemed like a very competent and intelligent woman.

A friend of Jane's called me one day and set up an appointment for counseling. I invited a good friend of mine (Mike Wright), whom I knew I could trust, to come with me. When I arrived at the house there were about a dozen people crowded into the living room. They were all concerned about Jane and curious about what I was going to do.

I began by asking Jane about her problem. She described her situation and what the psychiatrist had recommended. I asked her if she had been involved in the occult and if she used drugs. She answered "yes" to both questions. I have discovered that people who have tampered with the occult, no matter how slight, are often subject to demonic torment. This seems to be true even for Christians. The devil is a legalist and will use every opportunity to his advantage.

As I listened to Jane tell her own story, it seemed very apparent to me that she could have a demonic problem. Several warning signals usually include; bizarre behavior, occult involvement, strange religious ideas and practices, major family problems, unforgiveness, deep depression and suicidal tendencies. Jane had all of these. Therefore, I asked her if I could pray with her and she agreed. We started by seeking the Lord's forgiveness for disobedience and occult involvement. Then I led her in a prayer of forgiveness for all those she hated (see Matthew 6). I recommended she ask the Lord to deliver her after she removed all ties with the devil. Then I began to come against the evil spirits I suspected to be in her. One by one they manifested (took control of her) and in the name of Jesus, I drove them out. Some of the spirits included suicide, depression, insanity, fear, lust, pride and many others. It took several hours before we completed our session. When we ended, Jane was a different person. But I warned her that the demons would try to return and she would need to resist them in Jesus' name. She also needed to change her lifestyle so she would not fall into the same sins. Jane was set free. Several months later she came and testified that Jesus had set her free and now she was no longer nine different people but one.

Jane was only one of many who came requesting help. The Lord was the one who set them free, I was just the servant He used. But after a while I got tired of it. My family often came under demonic attack along with me and strange eerie things kept happening in our lives. Dealing with demons is dirty work and it's very controversial. People heard the stories of those who had been set free and they told other people, who told others. Soon I was overloaded with people wanting deliverance.

Therefore, one day I asked God to stop them from coming and for Him to use someone else. God answered that prayer. Soon the power was gone and so were the people seeking help. I knew I had displeased God and I continually asked for His forgiveness and for the miracles to return. Yet for three years all of heaven was silent toward me on this issue.

Then one day I received a phone call from Donna. "Den, there is a woman named Barb whom I think needs deliverance. Would you be willing to help her?"

"Yes!" I quickly responded.

This marked a turning point in my ministry. I met with Donna and Barb and another fine Christian woman named Mary Jo. As we listened to Barb's story of a life filled with rejection, insecurity, depression and fear, I began to sense a deep compassion for this victim of the enemy. At one point Barb hung her head and wept uncontrollably. Her life was a shambles. She was being tormented by invaders who were hindering her from enjoying life. At that moment, as I looked at this disheveled woman before me, I didn't care what any other pastors might say about the controversial nature of the deliverance ministry. I didn't care if the District Superintendent or the Bishop questioned the reality of demons in modern America. I just felt pity for this victim of the devil. As I looked down at her I got mad at the devil.

"You creep. I command every tormenting spirit in this woman to loose her now. You have no power over her any longer. Get out of her, in Jesus' name."

When it was all over Barb seemed like a different person, more confident and in control. The tears were gone, replaced with joy.

As I climbed into my car and drove away, I looked at the beautiful sunset and prayed, "Father, I'm ready. Use me to set the captives free. Send me out in the power of the Holy Spirit and I don't care how controversial it appears to other people. In Jesus' name, let's do it!"

42

THE CROSS

Wonderful things were happening in our two churches. People were being delivered, healed and converted to Christianity. We were discipling people and just starting a care group ministry. Even though everything was going great, I felt a tugging on my heart to leave. My dream of becoming an active duty chaplain was ever present in my thinking. I had gone through all the interviews with my denomination and they endorsed me for active duty with the Air Force. Over the years I had struggled with all the memories of Vietnam and decided that I didn't want to be in the Army on active duty. I wanted to be in the Air Force where it was safer. However, there weren't any openings in the Air Force, so my name was placed on a waiting list. Now everything was in place. I would continue to serve in the Army National Guard until a slot opened up with the Air Force on active duty.

However, I received several letters from denominational endorsing agents informing me that the chances of going Air Force were very slim. There just weren't any openings and the Air Force was even cutting back on the slots they previously had. The letter went on to say that there were openings with the Army. The decision was mine to make.

I had always wanted to be in the Air Force. I had previously served with the Marines and in the Army. Now I wanted to do something different. But with the cutbacks and the letters from my denomination encouraging me to switch to the Army, I wasn't sure what to do. So I prayed asking for God's wisdom. It took several sessions in prayer before I felt like I received an answer.

One day as I was praying in the sanctuary of the Climax church, I sensed the presence of God enter the room. Then this question penetrated my mind: "Would you be willing to serve as a Navy chaplain with the Marines?"

"THE NAVY?" I responded.

For the next two days I wrestled with that question. I don't like ships that spend so much of their time away from dry land. I don't like sharks, octopuses, whales or barracudas. It's dangerous on the ocean. If the storms or icebergs don't get you, the enemy will. Then it's a fight to survive in the water long enough to be rescued. Besides, I had already served for about five months on a ship in the Mediterranean. Added to those obstacles were the long separations from family. No, the Navy didn't sound like my kind of place. But I knew if God wanted me there He could help me deal with the obstacles. After two days of wrestling with the issue, I finally said "Yes" to God.

As I bowed before the Lord that day ready to submit to His will, He threw me a curve ball.

"If you are willing to serve Me in the Navy as a Chaplain then why won't you serve Me in the Army?"

God's question blew me away. In that moment, I saw how God had been opening doors of opportunity for me with the Army, but I was resisting His leading. I hated war and I was afraid to go back on the front lines where the action was. I thought the Air Force or even the Navy would be a safer alternative.

That day in the sanctuary on my knees before the Lord, He reminded me where my safety came from. It was not from tanks or buildings but from the Lord. My real question had to do with God's ability to protect me. It seemed ridiculous for me to even consider that the God who created the whole world in all of its wonder would not be able to protect me wherever I was; be that in a fox hole with the Army, on a ship at sea with the Navy, or on the flight line of an Air Force base.

"Father, forgive me for my arrogance. More than anything else I want Your will in my life. I am willing to serve You in the Army, Navy, Air Force, Marines or Coast Guard. Forgive me for trying to dictate to You. You are the Lord of my life. I am Your servant. Send me wherever You want me to go."

The Cross

About that time my friend from the Pentagon saw me at a Chaplain training event and said it wasn't too late to get in. I had just turned 39 and I only had until I was 40 to be accepted. Therefore, I filled out all the paperwork and took the physical examination needed for acceptance. Then I waited and prayed. Almost every night I walked out in my backyard and talked to the Lord about becoming a chaplain. From my perspective I knew it would take a miracle for me to be accepted. I was given my miracle.

When I informed my two churches that we would be leaving, there were a lot of tears shed. Things had been going so well that it was hard for some to understand. Even other National Guard chaplains questioned me on my decision. "You are so close to retirement, why mess it up by going on active duty?" My response was, "I feel like God is leading me in that direction."

In October of 1988, I left the pastorate to become an active duty chaplain. Our churches laid hands on us and sent us out as their missionaries to the military. A CROSS was now pinned on my uniform to identify me as a Protestant chaplain. The cross is a symbol for the sacrifice of Jesus. It is also a symbol of obedience unto death. All Christians are to take up their cross and follow Jesus. In that sense, the cross represents self-denial. I had to deny myself when I received my orders for Texas, a state not even on my dream sheet. Yet I was being assigned to one of the biggest Army bases in the Continuous United States, Fort Hood.

I was assigned to work with Division Artillery of the First Cavalry Division. There were five chaplains assigned to that brigade size force. My battalion was the first of the twentieth, usually referred to as the "BIG GUNS". It was called the big gun battalion because it had the largest gun of all the artillery weapons currently in use in the Army. While that fact set us apart in terms of the type of firepower we could provide, it had little effect on making us different from all other units in terms of the kinds of problems with which we had to deal. Most Army units struggled with drug and alcohol abuse, A.W.O.L., poor motivation, boredom, spouse and child abuse, high divorce rate, financial problems and continual problems with authority. For chaplains, that meant carrying a heavy counseling load. In most cases, the chaplain was the soldier's best friend. The chaplain had access to the commander and everyone else in the chain of command. Therefore, chaplains spend a lot of their time going to bat for soldiers with problems.

My duties as a chaplain included early morning physical fitness training (PT), attending staff briefings, counseling, preaching occasionally at the Red Team Chapel, pulling 24 hour duty at the hospital monitoring a crisis hotline, going to the field any time my soldiers did, and participating in other military functions. My basic philosophy of ministry while on active duty could be summed up in the slogan, "No Contact = No Impact", which meant that I needed to get out among the troops and not stay in my office waiting for people to drop in.

For my first six weeks at Ft. Hood I stayed with Chaplain Donnie and Annette Thrasher. They were so gracious in taking me into their home and making me a part of their family that I shall always be indebted to them. By mid-November Karen and the kids arrived. We rented an apartment for a couple of weeks until we were able to locate a house to rent. Karen was not sure that we should rent a house and so she prayed for a sign, like a rainbow. As we were looking at one particular house that I really liked, Karen went into one of the bedrooms and came out crying. For on the back of that bedroom door was a rainbow that a child had drawn on a piece of paper. Somehow it had been overlooked during the cleaning of the house. We knew it wasn't an accident. We decided to rent that house.

Inspired by the many answers to prayer in the lives of their parents, our children decided to pray specifically about friends. There were no children of similar ages on our street, but there was an empty house. Our children asked the Lord to give them some friends about the same age in that empty house across the street. About two weeks later someone did move into that house and we went next door to meet our new neighbors, Bob and Mary Giebner. We knew God had graciously answered our prayers when we met their three children (Jill, Josh, & Hilary) almost exactly the ages of our kids. Bob was a pilot on the new Apache helicopters. During some initial conversations we discovered that we had both been in Vietnam about the same time. Our children and our wives got acquainted and we quickly became friends. Soon after their arrival they asked us to take care of their kids because they had an emergency in the family and had to fly out right away. With pleasure we took them and for about a week became their adopted parents. We drew very close to the Giebner family that week.

When Bob and Mary arrived back at Ft. Hood we invited them to go with us to the Red Team Chapel and they took us up on it. Their attendance resulted in conversations about the Bible and Jesus. It wasn't long before the Giebner family decided to put their faith in Christ and we truly became "family" in the Lord.

During our time on active duty we were able to lead many people to Christ. People in the Army community were hurting and often looked for answers to make sense out of life. Jesus had given us the answers to our questions, so it was only natural that we shared with others what we had learned. As we did, people responded. It was especially fun to do this as a family. Even our children saw themselves as missionaries.

Another thing that was great for us was the decision we had made to homeschool our children. In the midst of our many moves, it helped to bring stability to our family. In addition, Karen had the joy of being involved in leading a homeschool support group. The group soon grew to over thirty families. Karen's teaching talents were stretched as she planned weekly excursions and workshops. It was a wonderful time for our whole family. We made many lifetime friends as a result of being involved in that group.

However, one of the things I didn't like about Army life was the extended times of separation because of field duty. One of those events took place the day after Thanksgiving in 1989, when I boarded a plane for NTC (National Training Center) in the Mojave Desert. We were practicing for desert warfare with the Russians. It was amazing to see how well tanks could hide in the desert. Our Task Force went out claiming we were going to wipe out everyone and instead the desert rats, who worked that terrain all the time, beat us in every battle but one.

From the Point to the Cross

Karen's brother, Jeff, had become a medical doctor in the Air Force, and was stationed at that time at George Air Force Base in southern California, not too far from where we were training. Before my time in the field we were able to get together for a meal at the officer's club. Jeff and his lovely wife Laurie, who was almost nine months pregnant at the time, must have been done in by that military food because she had her baby right after our get together. When I got out of the field on the other end of our training, I was able to sneak away to be with them and meet my new nephew, Brandon.

As a chaplain, field duty at NTC was an exciting ministry. "Every day is Sunday", was our slogan. We did worship services whenever and wherever we could. Usually it was off the back of trucks or tanks. I used taped Christmas music for the services to remind our men that back in the rest of the world everyone was preparing for Christmas. It was an effective ministry tool for soldiers who were otherwise totally blocked off from the normal sights and sounds of Christmas.

Our head chaplain for that operation was George Gardner. I admired George. He maintained his spirituality while at the same time being very proficient at his job. We had a great team of chaplains during that desert operation and it showed in the ministry we were able to provide. Larry Baldridge was another chaplain I had the privilege of working closely with in the desert. When it was all said and done the chaplains were reported to have done an outstanding job. We boarded our planes for home with our heads held high. We now felt confident about desert warfare. None of us had any idea that those skills would be tested in a real world situation before the next Christmas rolled around.

43

THE LEADING OF GOD

It felt great to be back home with my wife and family and to enjoy the comforts of modern life. We had a wonderful Christmas together and even invited about thirty soldiers over to our house to share it with us.

I really enjoyed ministry within my battalion. Though I missed my family and the comforts of modern life, I especially enjoyed ministry in the field.

However, it was a tough time to be in the military due to Congressional budget cuts, resulting in a rapid downsizing. Many chaplains would soon be out of a job as their slots would be eliminated. Competition for the remaining slots would be tough.

At Ft. Hood we had 72 full-time chaplains from many different denominational backgrounds. However, denominational differences were rarely a factor in hindering us from caring for soldiers and fulfilling duty assignments. Our problems had little to do with theology, but a lot to do with politics, power plays, and securing our own future. Some chaplains became so engrossed in playing political games that they lost their effectiveness as spiritual leaders. Somehow doing works to be seen by men and still being an effective minister of the Gospel just didn't jive. I refused to play political games. Therefore, I was not very popular.

As the New Year approached, I decided to spend extra time in prayer seeking the Lord's will for my life. This was a practice I had started in Bible College and one that has proven very beneficial over the years.

During that time of seeking the Lord's will for my life in the New Year, I sensed the Lord revealing to me that I was to get out of the Army. At first I wasn't sure that it was really God. I knew volunteers would be asked to leave the chaplaincy as job slots were being eliminated. However, my dream had been to be an active duty chaplain.

As I thought about it, I knew that above everything else I wanted to obey God. Though I enjoyed ministry in my battalion, I also thoroughly enjoyed ministry within a church setting. I'd learned the "grass isn't greener on the other side". Neither type of ministry was any better or more beneficial to God's kingdom. In the military, there had been opportunities to reach a great number of soldiers with the Gospel message. In the pastorate, however, there was a greater opportunity to build long term relationships. Ultimately, the most effective ministry for me could only be assured if I was right where God wanted me to be.

As I continued to pray, it seemed like the Lord said to me, *"In January of 1991 you will begin a doctorate program at Trinity Evangelical Divinity School in Deerfield, Illinois."*

I had wanted to begin a doctorate program for years, but was this just something I was making up in my mind? January 1991 seemed impossible since I had signed an initial three year commitment with the Army which wouldn't end until October 1991. I needed to know if this was really the leading of God.

"God, if this is really You, You're going to have to make it all happen. I'm willing to do my part but I need to know if this is really You. Show me that You're leading me by helping me to get out of the Army early. I would like to go back and pastor at least part time and I know most appointments to churches are given in the summer. Therefore, help me get out of the Army by this summer. I don't want to hurt my record, so help me to do this all honorably. (Pause) Lord, it would be nice if You would help me get accepted into the program at Trinity and I really need to get a computer before I go. (Pause) Lord, I don't know how I would finance such a deal, so it sure would be helpful if I had my car paid off. I would also like to get back into my old National Guard unit in Dowagiac. As a matter of fact, I would like to pastor a church in that area around Dowagiac so that it wouldn't be so far to drive to the Chicago area for school. One other thing, Lord, could You work on convincing Karen? She is not going to like this idea. If You could even go before us and prepare a couple of ladies in our new neighborhood who would become Karen's good friends, I sure would appreciate it. You know how important that is to her. And if You could do the same for my kids too, that would be great! I know this is a lot to ask but we need some miracles to prove to us that this is what we should do. Thanks, Lord. May Your will be done."

That prayer had a lot of impossible conditions that needed to be met. Some would call it a "fleece" prayer. That idea is actually based on a Biblical story about a man named Gideon, recorded in the book of Judges chapter six. God chose Gideon to lead the army of Israel into battle, but Gideon needed to know if this was truly God's will for him. My own paraphrase of their conversation goes something like this:

Gideon :	"You want me to go and do what?
GOD :	"Go and save Israel from the Midianites."
Gideon :	"Lord, I am not a warrior. How can I help Israel?"
GOD :	"Go mighty warrior...For I will be with you."
Gideon :	"OK, God, if this is really of You I'm going to place this fleece of wool out tonight and if You really want me to do this, then make the fleece wet tomorrow morning and all the ground dry."

When Gideon woke up the next day, the fleece was wet and the ground dry. Just to be sure it wasn't an accident, he asked God to reverse it the next night and make the fleece dry and the ground wet. In the morning it was as he requested. After convincing Gideon, God helped him to win a great military victory against unbeatable odds.

As I read that story, I figured if it was good enough for Gideon, then it was good enough for me. I believe that on most decisions God expects us to use the brain He's given us. The use of fleeces could easily be abused. However, in this life changing situation I knew I needed God's intervention to set up the details. Therefore, I felt that I needed God to guide me through a fleece.

The next hurdle would be confronting my wife with this message from the Lord. I have always liked new challenges but Karen is more hesitant.

She doesn't like change. Therefore, I cautiously approached her with this latest revelation.

"Karen, I've been talking with the Lord and I want you to know that something just might be coming down the pike. (Pause) I'm not positive but I think we might be getting out of the Army."

"WHAT?" Karen responded with fire in her eyes.
"I said I think God is leading us to get out of the Army."
"You mean YOU want to get out."
"Yes, it's true I do want to get out. But as I have been praying, I believe God has spoken to me to get out and pursue a Doctorate Degree at Trinity in Deerfield, Illinois, beginning in January of 1991."
"Well, God hasn't told me and I think you're wrong."
SILENCE.
"I'm going to pray against it." Karen added. "I love our life here. Our children love it."
"Karen, let me show you my diary which records my fleece with God."

Karen looked at the list of things I was asking God to do to prove to us that it was really His leading for us.

"I want to add to this list. Let's ask that both cars be paid off and that we come up with extra cash and . . ."

"Karen, I've already made a deal with God. I think you'll have to agree that if He does the things on my list it will be a miracle. And if He does we are going to follow His leading and get out."

As her final comment Karen added, "I still think you're wrong and I'm going to pray against it."

I believe that the husband is to be the leader in the family as the Bible indicates in Ephesians 5:22-33. Sometimes that means that I need to make decisions for my family that they may not agree with. This was one of those times. I realized that my wisdom, knowledge and foresight were very limited. God would have to prove that this was His leading beyond a shadow of a doubt because it was a major decision that would effect our whole family.

The very next day after my conversation with Karen my supervising Chaplain came up to me and said:

The Leading of God

"Chaplain Slattery, would you be interested in getting out of the Army early if it were possible?"

"YES!"

The Army was just beginning to reduce the number of soldiers on active duty and they were asking for volunteers to get out early. I submitted the paperwork and after personal interviews with those in command, I was given the OK. They asked me to put in writing the date I wanted to be released from active duty and I put down July 15, 1990. I figured that would give me time to get my affairs in order. Two weeks after saying "YES" my packet had been approved and sent through channels up to the Pentagon.

Next I contacted the Methodist Church in Michigan and asked them to find me a Church. In the Methodist system this is all done through appointments by the Bishop and District Superintendents. They told me they would do what they could.

I also made contact with the Michigan National Guard to see if I could work with them as a reserve chaplain again. I was told there were no slots. Having served as a Chaplain in Indiana, I checked with them and discovered that they had an open slot in South Bend, just over the border from Michigan.

With the pieces beginning to fall into place, I applied at Trinity for the doctorate program. Before I received word from them we were hit by a bad hail storm. I stood by the window that night and watched the hail pound my car. That week I contacted my insurance company and they were willing to give me a check for the damage of almost $2,000 made out to the firm that financed my car. My car was now paid off and yet still in good working order.

With each day that passed Karen was becoming more and more convinced that God was truly leading us to get out of the Army. In the meantime, we were offered a church in Dowagiac. We met with the board and looked at the parsonage while we were on vacation. It even had an unoccupied bunny hutch in back which was an answer to my children's prayers.

While in the Michigan area I attended a Billy Graham training conference at Wheaton College. One day there was a message for me to call Chaplain Mike Brallier in Michigan. When I called he had an urgent message for me.

"Don't sign up as a Chaplain with Indiana. The 246 Armory in Dowagiac just opened up and we want you to take it."

Praise God! Every request was answered, including the computer. Someone sent us some money and we found a catalog for computers. The price matched and we bought it. One final desire I had was that I could get all my teeth fixed before leaving active duty. According to the dentists I needed four crowns and gum surgery. They told me it was impossible to get it all done before July 2 but I kept praying and miracles kept happening. When the second of July arrived, my surgery had been completed and I had four new crowns. I'd learned an important lesson having to do with Psalm 37:4, which says, *"Delight yourself in the Lord and He will give you the desires of your heart."*

On July 2, 1990, we loaded our moving van, hooked the car to the rear, put the bunnies in a traveling cage and drove away from Ft. Hood without any regrets. God had proven to us beyond a shadow of a doubt that this was indeed His will.

44

YELLOW RIBBONS

In August of 1990, I had to go for training with the 246 Armor to Mississippi. When we arrived at Camp Shelby many of the units were called upon to take part in Operation Desert Shield which was already in progress in Saudi Arabia. Had I been delayed just two weeks on getting out of the Army, I too would have been in the desert, since most of Ft. Hood went to support that operation. My National Guard unit, the 246 Armor, was not called upon to go, although it came close. No one knew that I had prayed to God after my second tour in Vietnam asking that I not have to fight in another war. I know the realities of war and I hate it. However, I love being a chaplain in the Army. God answered my prayer in a marvelous way.

In January of 1991, I began my Doctorate program at Trinity. On January 16th, I went out to eat with my professor and several other students. As we waited for our dinner to arrive someone yelled, "We're at war!" People from all over the restaurant rushed over to the TV in order to watch our planes bombing Iraq. Tracers and explosions were lighting up the skies. I felt strange as I stood there watching that scene. It was as if God tapped me on the shoulder and spoke into my ear.

"Son, you are right where you belong. Did I not tell you that in January of 1991 you would be at Trinity working on your Doctorate?"

From the Point to the Cross

I was in awe. I had no idea this would happen. We were at war. The next two months were very difficult for me. I found myself crying while watching the news. One day as I drove through a small town in southwestern Michigan tears filled my eyes. Everywhere I looked I saw yellow ribbons. It said to me that these people supported the troops. My mind flashed back to the lack of support I received during my two tours in Vietnam. No one put out yellow ribbons. There were no celebrations or parades. No one seemed to care. The scars were opened up again during Desert Storm. I know the same thing happened to Vietnam vets all across the country. The wounds of our heart that we thought were healed were opened up again and many of us became very emotional.

Al Kickert, one of the neat men in the Silver Creek United Methodist Church, said he would like to see me greet some of the men in my old unit when they got home. At first the idea seemed far fetched. I had no idea when any of the units were coming home nor did anyone else. But Al started a collection and the Silver Creek Church graciously sent us to Ft. Hood for a vacation.

On April 8th, 1991, we were at Ft. Hood and it just so happened to be the day several flights of soldiers from the First Cavalry Division were arriving. Several chaplains I knew, as well as some men from my old units, were on those planes. What a divine coincidence that I was able to greet those soldiers and participate in a wonderful welcome home celebration. Over the loud speakers they played the song, *I'm Proud to be an American*. With tears in my eyes, I walked away from the celebration thinking this is the way we should always welcome our returning heroes, with the bands playing and the crowds shouting. These men risked their lives for their country. They had a job to do and they did it right. Maybe America had learned something from Vietnam after all. This was a day to be proud.

As I turned to get one last look at the sight of families hugging each other, God gave me a revelation. I saw in my mind's eye a picture of a huge army in heaven with millions of people gathered together. The attention of everyone was on the newcomers just arriving. I was one of the newcomers. People were shouting happily and clapping their hands as we entered. From all directions people were saying, "You did it! Good job! Way to go! You were faithful to the end!" Tears were freely flowing down my cheeks.

Then I sensed God saying to me, *"This celebration here today is nothing compared to what will happen when the soldiers of Christ enter heaven. I know you are proud to be an American on this day, but I want you to be proud that you are called by My Name. Be proud that you are a Christian."*

I am, Lord. I am proud to be a Christian. Thanks for making me part of Your family. Help me to be faithful to the end, so that I can enter heaven with my head held high and hear those words that I so long to hear,

"WELCOME HOME, MY GOOD AND FAITHFUL SERVANT."

EPILOGUE

The story you have just read is true, told from my perspective. I would hope that while reading this book you have discovered that I am not a perfect person, even though I once prayed to receive Jesus as my Lord and Savior. Jesus is the only perfect person. For the rest of us, perfection in this life is like a mirage in the desert that is always just out of reach. He is still working on me. Therefore, I still make mistakes and struggle with my old nature that is bent on rebellion and sin. I have done many things in my life that I regret. However, I can't undo the wrong, I can only seek the Lord's forgiveness. It still amazes me that God uses imperfect people for His own glory.

My story is really His-story. It's the story of how God changed a pleasure seeking, atheistic, sinner into a new creature in Christ. It is also the story of how He took a hardened Marine pointman and turned him into an Army Chaplain. I take the blame for all my wrong decisions, failures, and sins. I give God all the credit for anything good that He has been able to do through me.

In II Corinthians 5:20-21 we find these words:

> *"We are therefore Christ's ambassadors, as though God were making His appeal through us. We implore you on Christ's behalf: Be reconciled to God. God made Him who had no sin to be sin for us, so that in Him we might become the righteousness of God."*

God uses people whom He has touched to reach out to other people who need His touch. All I can share with you is how God touched my life. If you need Him in your life, I encourage you to put this book down and seek the living God. You may not see Him but He can see you. God helps those who ask for His help, so ask. He is always only a prayer away.

God loves you and so do I!

Den Slattery

RECOMMENDED BOOKS

One of the common requests that I frequently receive is to recommend some book that might help someone deal with a particular problem that they are struggling with. On other occasions, I am even asked if I would recommend a good Christian novel or biography. Therefore, I have put together the following list of books that deal with a variety of subjects which I hope will help someone.

ABOUT VIETNAM
"Nam Vet", (Making Peace with Your Past) by Chuck Dean
"Beyond The Glory", by William Kimball
"Pointman", by William Kimball & Roger Helle
"If I Make My Bed in Hell", by Chaplain John Porter
"Prison to Praise", by Chaplain Merlin Carothers
"When Hell Was In Session" (POW in Vietnam) by Jeremiah Denton Jr.
"Beyond Combat" by Chaplain James Hutchens

BASICS OF THE FAITH
"Essential Practices" by Den Slattery & Gary Wales
"Essential Truths" by Den Slattery & Gary Wales
"Evidence That Demands A Verdict" by Josh McDowell
"The Case for Christ" by Lee Strobel
"The Case for Faith" by Lee Strobel
"The Case for a Creator" by Lee Strobel

BREAKING BAD HABITS
"Bondage Breaker" by Neil Anderson
"Freedom from Addictions" by Neil Anderson
"The Jesus Factor" by David Manuel
"The Useful Lie" by William Playfair MD

PRAYER
"Destined For the Throne" by Paul Billheimer
"Celebration of Discipline" by Richard Foster
"Let Prayer Change Your Life" by Becky Tirabassi
"Too Busy Not To Pray" by Bill Hybels
"The Prayer of Jabez" by Bruce Wilkinson
"The Hour That Changes the World" by Dick Eastman
"The Incredible Power of Prayer" by David Balsiger
"Too Busy Not to Pray" by Bill Hybels

MISSIONS
"Revolution in World Missions" by K.P. Yohannan
"Hudson Taylor's Spiritual Secret" by Dr. & Mrs. Howard Taylor
"Touch the World through Prayer" by Wesley Duewel
"Invasion of Other Gods" by David Jeremiah
"Is That Really You God?" By Lorren Cunningham

EVANGELISM
"Evangelism Explosion" by D. James Kennedy
"Witnessing Without Fear" by Bill Bright
"Hell's Best Kept Secret" by Ray Comfort
"Conspiracy of Kindness" by Steve Sjogren
"Nothing to Do but To Save Souls" by Robert E. Coleman
"Laboring In the Harvest" by Leroy Eims

DISCIPLESHIP
"The Master Plan of Evangelism" by Robert E. Coleman
"Jesus Christ Disciplemaker" by Bill Hull
"The Lost Art of Making Disciples" by Leroy Eims
"The Purpose Driven Church" by Rick Warren

DEFENDING THE CHRISTIAN FAITH
"The Roots of Evil" by Norman Geisler
"God, I Don't Understand" by Ken Boa
"A Ready Defense" by Josh McDowell
"The Lie"by Ken Ham
"Know What You Believe" by Paul Little

Recommended Books

"Evidence That Demands a Verdict" by Josh McDowell
"Faith Training" by Joe White

SPIRITUAL WARFARE
"Deliver Us from Evil" by Don Basham
"Expelling Demons" by Derek Prince
"Deliverance for Children and Teens" by Bill Banks
"Bondage Breaker" by Neil Anderson
"Spiritual Warfare" by Timothy Warner
"Three Battlegrounds" by Francis Frangipane

MARRIAGE & FAMILY
"The Total Woman" by Marabel Morgan
"The Blessing" by Gary Smalley & John Trent
"Love for a Lifetime" By James Dobson
"Me? Obey Him?" By Elizabeth Rice Hanford
"Tender Warrior" by Stu Weber
"Pointman" by Steve Farr
"The New Dare to Discipline" by James Dobson
"Faith Training" by Joe White

ATTITUDES
"The Power of Positive Students" by William Mitchell
"Raising Positive Kids in a Negative World" by Zig Zigler
"Right Thinking" by Bill Hull
"Thinking For a Change" by John Maxwell

HEALTH - - HEALING - - DIET
"A Cancer Battle Plan" by Anne Fraham
"Reclaim Your Health" by Anne Fraham
"Are You Sick & Tired?" By Mary Ruth Swope
"Body for Life" by Bill Phillips
"Where Is God When It Hurts?" By Philip Yancey
"When God Doesn't Make Sense" by James Dobson
"Reversing Heart Disease" by Julian Whitaker MD
"Reversing Diabetes" by Julian Whitaker MD
"How To Have A Healing Ministry" by C. Peter Wagner

GOOD BOOKS FOR THE METHODIST CHURCH
"Essential Truths" by Den Slattery & Gary Wales
"Essential Practices" by Den Slattery & Gary Wales
"And Are We Yet Alive" by Richard Wilke
"New Life for Dying Churches" by Rose Sims
"Be a People Person" by John Maxwell
"Multiplication" by Tommy Barnett
"Where Do We Go From Here?" By Ralph Neighbour
"The Purpose Driven Church" by Rick Warren

GOOD CHRISTIAN BIOGRAPHIES
"Prison to Praise" by Merlin Carothers
"The Calling" by Brother Andrew
"The Cross and the Switchblade" by David Wilkerson
"Is That Really You God?" By Lorren Cunningham
"Through Gates of Splendor" by Elizabeth Elliot
"Run Baby Run" by Nicky Cruz
"The Autobiography of George Muller" by George Muller
"The Navigator"(Story of Dawson Trotman) by Robert Foster
"Betrayed" (A Jewish family becomes Christians) by Stan Telchin
"Born Again" by Chuck Colson

GOOD CHRISTIAN NOVELS
"The Stirring" by Robert Moeller
"This Present Darkness" by Frank Peretti
"Piercing the Darkness" by Frank Peretti
"The Third Millennium" by Paul Meier
"The Testament" by John Grisham
"Gideon's Gift" by Karen Kingsbury
"Full Draw (The Hunter) by Steve Chapman
"Blink" by Ted Dekker

DEN'S OTHER BOOKS

Life Goes On picks up Den's story where *From the Point to the Cross* leaves off. It could have been called *Lessons From Life* because each chapter deals with a lesson Den has learned. From breaking bad habits to discovering that the Devil does win a few battles. This book will make you cry during one chapter and laugh in the next. Some have even said it helped them grow.

"I have known Chaplain Slattery for 13 years and have watched him advance through the ranks from Chaplain Canidate to Major in the Michigan Army National Guard. This book is a candid review of his frustrations and successes as he experienced the Lord's leading through a sometimes perilous and frequently exciting life."
 Chaplain (COL) Jay Pruim (Michigan Army National Guard)

"I read this book in one day and thoroughly enjoyed it! Den writes in a way that draws people into his life experiences. My favorite chapter was Thumb Sucking.*"*
 Chris Lubitz (Texas)

From the Point to the Cross

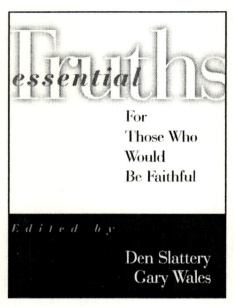

What should we believe? In a world where everything seems relative, how can we discover the truth to base our life upon? Fifteen different authors will help to answer these questions. This book will help you study the issues of faith with Robert E. Coleman, David Seamands, Terry Teykl, Robert Tuttle, James Heidinger and ten other gifted people.

These books can be obtained by calling 1-800 451- READ

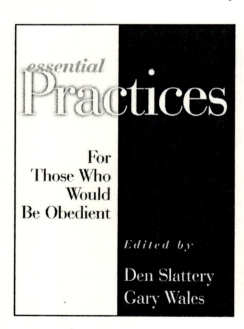

It is not enough for most people to just know facts, they need to know how to live. What are the essential things that Christians should be doing? Let these effective communicators help you with the practice of your faith. Authors include, Henry Gariepy, Gil Stafford, Warren Benson, Janice Shaw Crouse, Gus Gustafson, and ten other writers.

Printed in the United States
18237LVS00003B/325